COLLECTED POEMS

Collected Poems
1956–1994

THOMAS KINSELLA

Oxford   New York

OXFORD UNIVERSITY PRESS

1996

Oxford University Press, Walton Street, Oxford OX2 6DP

Oxford New York
Athens Auckland Bangkok Bogota Bombay
Buenos Aires Calcutta Cape Town Dar es Salaam
Delhi Florence Hong Kong Istanbul Karachi
Kuala Lumpur Madras Madrid Melbourne
Mexico City Nairobi Paris Singapore
Taipei Tokyo Toronto

and associated companies in
Berlin Ibadan

Oxford is a trade mark of Oxford University Press

Collected Poems 1956–1994 first published
in Oxford Poets as an
Oxford University Press paperback 1996

British Library Cataloguing in Publication Data
Data available

Library of Congress Cataloging in Publication Data
Data available

ISBN 0–19–282526–7

Typeset by Rowland Phototypesetting Limited
Printed in Hong Kong

Contents

COLLECTED POEMS

POEMS (1956);
ANOTHER SEPTEMBER (1958)

Echoes

Alone we make symbols of love
Out of echoes its lack makes in an empty word.
Inaccessible softness of breast or voice in the dove
Or high gull grace are what we are thinking of,
The poise in quality of a bird.
Time must pare such images to the heart.
Love I consider a difficult, scrupulous art.

A drumming of feet on a lake
When a stretched word touches the meaning like a swan
Points in the vanishing whisper of its wake
The course of argument that love must take
Until word and image are gone.
Out of a certain silence it may bring
The softer dove or a skylit glitter of wing.

Across the deepest speech,
When what is said is less than what is heard,
Gift to the shaken giver melts into each,
Receipt on the lips alights and returns to teach
What further words can be spared
Till graven language centres love with quiet
More full than spoken gesture can supply it.

So, much that the instant needs
Being faded token of what the next replaces,
An echo deepens as the past recedes;
Words like swans are swallowed into the reeds
With lapping airs and graces.
Speechless white necks dip in the fugal pause
When streaming images transfigure the dove that was.

3

What beats in its flaming throat
Or under its plumes, or what transfigures its flight
—A detail of light—what inexplicable mote
Drifts in the slanted shaft where loves are afloat
Flowers in no single sight;
In composite hearts there sings a full repose:
Mute splendour of a breast-soft, sea-graced close.

Test Case

Readier than flags rippling in the sun
To turn tragic in elegiac weathers,
More striking, forked and longer than lightning,
Is the heroic agenda, full of frightening
Things to kill or love or level down—
A man's life, magnified with monumental bothers.

Naked save for the skin of a preferably
Ferocious beast, pulling down roofs
Seriously to demonstrate some fact,
His queer quality is noticed—direct
Approach, statuesque faith—clearly he
Is unforgettable. Events will circle him with graves,

Curious to discover how far in given
Conditions a human attribute
May be goaded, what ultimate in grief
Can be tolerated for a belief,
What is utter love, how forgiving
Is degradation, what justice would rather die than commit.

In some kingdom his powers will be trapped
Formally, his special innocence
Quiver under his dilemma's vicious
Tensions and be torn to pieces,
His vital next move be stopped
For close study, and chronicles' titles fill with the news.

His native village, vaguely honoured
And confused by stories newly arriving,
Would have a little of minor value to add
—Anecdotes to charm students of his mad
Bleeding retreat to a stoic beloved,
The famous towering Death already avalanching.

The Travelling Companion

Why it was necessary to fumble out of the dark
Is nothing, nothing to how, having let in
    Light on the blind turmoil, it was possible
That these two starved jaws of the will,
    Naturally ravenous, should guide their ravening.

Yet balanced, snarling on claws, a fertile tension
Stretched its brightening muscles, sniffed and made
    Off in a carnal wonder, prowled with the hungry,
Panicked with alert deer, preyed in the sky,
    Skittered brilliantly across a still glade,

Marched over murderous plains to the ocean with savages,
On a crowded headland beat with a thousand hearts
    Knotted in fear of the narrow boats at its foot,
Came through the shrill distress of disturbed ledges
    With stern invaders, surfing ashore for good.

Entirely happy in battle, towards all warriors
It flashed out of the dust: entirely partial
    In bullet's bark, departing, and smack, arriving,
Displayed to satisfaction, in a matter of mirrors,
    How concerned the dead are with survivors

And that there is no discrimination;
Embarked from the quay when nocturnal brass, on behalf
    Of arc-white, wounded regiments, thanked their stars
And, far at sea, lies fumbling with packed blasts
    While the halls of night are slowly filling with force.

5

Night Songs

1

Now, as I sink in sleep,
My heart is cut down,
Nothing—poetry nor love—
Achieving.

*

Turns again in my room,
The crippled leopard.
Paw-pad, configured
Yellow light of his eyes,
Pass, repass, repass.

Quiet, my hand; he is tame.

Soon, while I dream, will step
And stir the sunken dawn.

2

Before I woke there entered in
A woman with a golden skin
    That tangled with the light.
A tang of orchards climbed the stair
And dwindled in the waxen air,
    Crisping the midnight,
And the white pillows of my bed
On apple-tasted darkness fed.
    Weakened with appetite
Sleep broke like a dish wherein
A woman lay with golden skin.

Midsummer

Hereabouts the signs are good.
Propitious creatures of the wood
    After their fashion
Have pitied and blessed before our eyes.
All unpremeditated lies
    Our scattered passion.

Flowers whose name I do not know
Make happy signals to us. O
    Did ever bees
Stumble on such a quiet before!
The evening is a huge closed door
    And no one sees

How we, absorbed in our own art,
Have locked ourselves inside one heart,
    Grown silent and,
Under beech and sacred larch,
Watched as though it were an arch
    That heart expand.

Something that for this long year
Had hid and halted like a deer
    Turned marvellous,
Parted the tragic grasses, tame,
Lifted its perfect head and came
    To welcome us.

We have, dear reason, of this glade
An endless tabernacle made,
    An origin.
Well for whatever lonely one
Will find this right place to lay down
    His desert in.

Soft, to your Places

Soft, to your places, animals.
Your legendary duty calls.
        It is, to be
Lucky for my love and me
        And yet we have seen that all's
A fiction that is heard of love's difficulty.

And what if the simple primrose show
That mighty work went on below
        Before it grew
A moral miracle for us two?
        Since of ourselves we know
Beauty to be an easy thing, this will do.

But O when beauty's brought to pass
Will Time set down his hour-glass
        And rest content,
His hand upon that monument?
        Unless it is so, alas
That the heart's calling is but to go naked and diffident.

Soft, to your places, love; I kiss
Because it is, because it is.

A Lady of Quality

In hospital where windows meet
With sunlight in a pleasing feat
        Of airy architecture
My love has sweets and grapes to eat,
The air is like a laundered sheet,
        The world's a varnished picture.

Books and flowers at her head
Make living-quarters of her bed
        And give a certain style

To our pillow-chat, the nonsense said
To bless the room from present dread
    Just for a brittle while.

For obvious reasons we ignore
The leaping season out-of-door,
    Light lively as a ferret,
Woodland walks, a crocused shore,
The transcendental birds that soar
    And tumble in high spirit

While under this hygienic ceiling
Where my love lies down for healing
    Tiny terrors grow,
Reflected in a look, revealing
That her care is spent concealing
    What, perhaps, I know.

'Ended and done with' never ceases,
Constantly the heart releases
    Wild geese to the past.
Look, how they circle poignant places,
Falling to sorrow's fowling-pieces
    With soft plumage aghast.

We may regret, and must abide.
Grief, the hunter's, fatal stride
    Among the darkening hearts
Has gone too long on either side.
Our trophied love must now divide
    Into its separate parts

And you go down with womankind
Who in her beauty has combined
    And focused human hungers,
With country ladies who could wind
A nation's love-affair with mind
    Around their little fingers,

While I communicate again
Recovered order to my pen
    To find a further answer
As, having looked all night in vain,
A weary prince will sigh and then
    Take a familiar dancer.

Now the window's turning dark
And ragged rooks across the Park
    Mix with branches; all
The clocks about the building mark
The hour. The random is at work
    Between us: two petals fall.

A train lifts up a lonely cry . . .
Our fingertips together lie
    Upon the counterpane.
It will be hard, it seems, and I
Would wish my heart to justify
    What qualities remain.

Fifth Sunday After Easter

April's sweet hand in the margins betrayed
Her character in late cursive daffodils.
A gauche mark, but beautiful; a maid.

Nostalgia in the sun . . . When the breeze stills,
The white parchment of the light—the cover
Her declaration came in—touches the breath
Faintly with rakish, innocent perfume.
                        Love her:
For her mistiming, for her longings, for her early death.

An Ancient Ballet

In the deep reaches of the night
The ticking stars keep order
That when the sleepless border
On marvel they shall sleep light.

This manner is the moon's:
Her silver hours are spent avoiding
The quiet clouds and their colliding
Over untended towns

That no eyes be raised her way.
Yet, such is her sleeplessness,
The morale of the heavens is
Distracted for us, if beautifully.

She draws our gazes thronging
Into the figured void
Her light feet deck, where we forget
We know her power is our longing

And I think that her stare discovers
Only what we pretend,
That the moon is lovely, but will descend
Through the night's honest endeavours.

It looked so when her face filled
My window one endless hour.
Brightly her darkness downpoured
Delusion, radiantly skilled.

Presently this room,
Much used for music, lined with books,
Where a faith died and a little lacks
—And once a panther came—

Disengaged, as the lunar curtain
Swung, its serious dancers from
Their stations and their time.
That they had loved is certain

As that in their wordlessness
They danced until I loved
And wove until they left
With their light feet such logic as,

Cleaving the eyes, laid waste
This pillow with my tears, my joy.
That mastering huge sky-
Stare, downstreaming, witnessed!

All about her lit as though
Blood rang, marvels toiled.
Close at heart there sailed
A stately vast plateau.

Yet I died, I died
The light death as I lay. My watch
Matched my wrist in the dark, searched
Awhile under the tide

Down to the salt still water
Where quietly, for miles,
Time lowers its twinkling shells
To a freighted bed, to a travelled floor.

Of time, of longing. Their recorder
Sleeps and they unite.
In the deep reaches of the night
The ticking stars keep order.

The Monk

He tramped in the fading light
Of a late February day
Between hedges stiff with the wind.

His boots trod stone and clay.
His blown habit swung
In the wet daylight's decay.

A spade across his shoulder
Slanted into the sky.
Sunk in the cowl his quiet eye.

A sense of scrubbed flesh in the path;
A thought of washing in cold hours
When dreams are scrubbed off

In a chill room, huge flowers,
Night blooms, accidentally plucked,
Each dawn devours;

Of a haggard taste in the mouth
Savouring in death a tide of light,
Spring in February night.

Baggot Street Deserta

Lulled, at silence, the spent attack.
The will to work is laid aside.
The breaking-cry, the strain of the rack,
Yield, are at peace. The window is wide
On a crawling arch of stars, and the night
Reacts faintly to the mathematic
Passion of a cello suite
Plotting the quiet of my attic.
A mile away the river toils
Its buttressed fathoms out to sea;
Tucked in the mountains, many miles
Away from its roaring outcome, a shy
Gasp of waters in the gorse
Is sonneting origins. Dreamers' heads
Lie mesmerised in Dublin's beds
Flashing with images, Adam's morse.

A cigarette, the moon, a sigh
Of educated boredom, greet
A curlew's lingering threadbare cry
Of common loss. Compassionate,

I add my call of exile, half-
Buried longing, half-serious
Anger and the rueful laugh.
We fly into our risk, the spurious.

Versing, like an exile, makes
A virtuoso of the heart,
Interpreting the old mistakes
And discords in a work of Art
For the One, a private masterpiece
Of doctored recollections. Truth
Concedes, before the dew, its place
In the spray of dried forgettings Youth
Collected when they were a single
Furious undissected bloom.
A voice clarifies when the tingle
Dies out of the nerves of time:
Endure and let the present punish.
Looking backward, all is lost;
The Past becomes a fairy bog
Alive with fancies, double crossed
By pad of owl and hoot of dog,
Where shaven, serious-minded men
Appear with lucid theses, after
Which they don the mists again
With trackless, cotton-silly laughter;
Secretly a swollen Burke
Assists a decomposing Hare
To cart a body of good work
With midnight mutterings off somewhere;
The goddess who had light for thighs
Grows feet of dung and takes to bed,
Affronting horror-stricken eyes,
The marsh bird that children dread.

I nonetheless inflict, endure,
Tedium, intracordal hurt,
The sting of memory's quick, the drear
Uprooting, burying, prising apart
Of loves a strident adolescent

Spent in doubt and vanity.
All feed a single stream, impassioned
Now with obsessed honesty,
A tugging scruple that can keep
Clear eyes staring down the mile,
The thousand fathoms, into sleep.

Fingers cold against the sill
Feel, below the stress of flight,
The slow implosion of my pulse
In a wrist with poet's cramp, a tight
Beat tapping out endless calls
Into the dark, as the alien
Garrison in my own blood
Keeps constant contact with the main
Mystery, not to be understood.
Out where imagination arches
Chilly points of light transact
The business of the border-marches
Of the Real, and I—a fact
That may be countered or may not—
Find their privacy complete.

My quarter-inch of cigarette
Goes flaring down to Baggot Street.

Tête à Tête

Try subtlety. 'I was in love all May
Not with you, really, but with You-in-Me.'

Better a simple pledge. Her clouded sight
Silenced the window table where they sat.

His play with her unsureness altered to
A faint compunction as she poured his tea.

Their happiness when they assured each other
Made neither happy to have faith in either.

Last time they spoke it was with fumbled feeling,
The station deafening, their voices failing.

Pause en Route

Death, when I am ready, I
Shall come; drifting where I drown,
Falling, or by burning, or by
Sickness, or by striking down.

Nothing you can do can put
My coming aside, nor what I choose
To come like—holy, broken or but
An anonymity—refuse.

But when I am ready be
What figure you will, bloodily dressed
Or with arms held gauzily
In at my door from the tempest.

And, if your task allow it, let
The ceaseless waters take us as
One soul conversing and, if it
Deny, let that civility pass.

Little, now as then, we know
How I shall address you or
You me. Embarrassment could go
Queerly with us, scavenger.

Nothing sure but that the brave
And proud you stopped I will not sing,
Knowing nothing of you save
A final servant functioning.

An Outdoor Gallery

Life was a mute wrenching of the heart,
A wound in the red roof of the mouth. Often
The very accomplishment of its bitterness
Insisted one should smile and, smiling, accept.

Rain without structure fell from a sky ill-kept
Sighing: 'If you are going you are going
And if you stay you stay, but you will change.
The place you change in is where you are strangest.'

Nowhere is stranger than the familiar—given
The intervention of a window-pane.
New love is reminiscent, like a plan,
Of loves you altered on before. Here, therefore.

Love, so regarded, nervous of rapture, placed
Item after item of beauty behind her.
Softly the lime of her own beauty traced
A structure in the rain. The sky grew kinder.

Over the mountain tops the night demurely
Loosened a clasp, opened her treasure trove.
Who would not give his ages for one star
To fix where it is warmest, on the tongue?

Climbing a star-lit mountain, Man With Beard
Greeted in gladness not transfiguration
But, for a while, himself, a Man With Lute,
And gave his soul up for the gift of thanks.

In the Ringwood

As I roved out impatiently
Good Friday with my bride
To drink in the rivered Ringwood
The draughty season's pride
A fell dismay held suddenly
Our feet on the green hill-side.

The yellow Spring on Vinegar Hill,
The smile of Slaney water,
The wind that swept the Ringwood,
Grew dark with ancient slaughter.
My love cried out and I beheld her
Change to Sorrow's daughter.

17

'Ravenhair, what rending
Set those red lips a-shriek,
And dealt those locks in black lament
Like blows on your white cheek,
That in your looks outlandishly
Both woe and fury speak?'

As sharp a lance as the fatal heron
There on the sunken tree
Will strike in the stones of the river
Was the gaze she bent on me.
Oh her robe into her right hand
She gathered grievously.

'Many times the civil lover
Climbed that pleasant place,
Many times despairing
Died in his love's face,
His spittle turned to vinegar,
Blood in his embrace.

Love that is every miracle
Is torn apart and rent.
The human turns awry
The poles of the firmament.
The fish's bright side is pierced
And good again is spent.

Though every stem on Vinegar Hill
And stone on the Slaney's bed
And every leaf in the living Ringwood
Builds till it is dead
Yet heart and hand, accomplished,
Destroy until they dread.

Dread, a grey devourer,
Stalks in the shade of love.
The dark that dogs our feet
Eats what is sickened of.
The End that stalks Beginning
Hurries home its drove.'

I kissed three times her shivering lips.
I drank their naked chill.
I watched the river shining
Where the heron wiped his bill.
I took my love in my icy arms
In the Spring on Ringwood Hill.

King John's Castle

Not an epic, being not loosely architectured,
    But with epic force, setting the head spinning
With the taut flight earthward of its bulk, King John's
    Castle rams fast down the county of Meath.
This in its heavy ruin. New, a brute bright plateau,
    It held speechless under its cold a whole province of Meath.

Now the man-rot of passages and broken window-casements,
    Vertical drops chuting through three storeys of masonry,
Draughty spiral stairways decaying in the depths,
    Are a labyrinth in the medieval dark. Intriguers
Who prowled here once, into the waiting arms
    Of their own monster, revisit the blowing dust.

Life, a vestigial chill, sighs along the tunnels
    Through the stone face. The great collapsed rooms, the mind
Of the huge head, are dead. Views open inward
    On empty silence; a chapel-shelf, moss-grown, unreachable.
King John directs at the river a grey stare, who once
    Viewed the land in a spirit of moderation and massacre.

Contemplatives, tiny as mice moving over the green
    Mounds below, might take pleasure in the well
Of quiet there, the dark foundations near at hand.
    Up here where the wind sweeps bleakly, as though in
        remembrance
Against our own tombstones, the brave and great might gather.
    For the rest, this is not their fortress.

Clarence Mangan

Sometimes, charting the heroes and animals of night-time,
Sudden unhappinesses would bewilder me,
Strayed in the long void of youth
Where nothing is understood.

Later, all mankind calling,
I, being anxious, eager to please, shouted my fear
That something was wrong.

Back to a wall, facing tumultuous talking faces,
Once I lost the reason for speech. My heart was taken,
Stretched with terror by only a word a mouth had uttered.

Long I waited to know what naked meeting
Would come with what was moving behind my eyes
And desolating what I touched.

Over a glass, or caught in lamplight,
Caught on the edge of act, my hand
Is suddenly stopped and fills with waiting.

Out of the shadows behind my laughter
Surgical fingers come
And I am strapped to a table.

Pitiless, again I ply the knife.

Another September

Dreams fled away, this country bedroom, raw
With the touch of the dawn, wrapped in a minor peace,
Hears through an open window the garden draw
Long pitch black breaths, lay bare its apple trees,
Ripe pear trees, brambles, windfall-sweetened soil,
Exhale rough sweetness against the starry slates.
Nearer the river sleeps St John's, all toil
Locked fast inside a dream with iron gates.

Domestic Autumn, like an animal
Long used to handling by those countrymen,
Rubs her kind hide against the bedroom wall
Sensing a fragrant child come back again
—Not this half-tolerated consciousness
That plants its grammar in her yielding weather
But that unspeaking daughter, growing less
Familiar where we fell asleep together.

Wakeful moth-wings blunder near a chair,
Toss their light shell at the glass, and go
To inhabit the living starlight. Stranded hair
Stirs on the still linen. It is as though
The black breathing that billows her sleep, her name,
Drugged under judgment, waned and—bearing daggers
And balances—down the lampless darkness they came,
Moving like women: Justice, Truth, such figures.

O Rome

O Rome thou art, at coffee break, O Rome
Thou also art a town of staring clerks,
Staring the azure window at mid-morning,
Commemorating something in a daze.

Dissociated from the flesh, upright
In attitude, they sit like organ pipes
Stale vapours of antiquity sigh through.
Each simple, all in stock-still harmony.

Death and the Professor

Our breed of trinket-burying avatars
Shrank to the cyst's confines, nosed their stiff shins.
You moved the muddy spade with open mind,
Slitting the hill of myth, and bled out truth.

Those bones behind museum glass, those antique
Bent militiamen remembered you
Who poked old ramparts with a walking stick
Thinking of graveyards. Godspeed underground.

Young men and women who looked up to you
Stand in their rubber boots a while forgetting
The skulls and joints they varnished and made safe,
The dusted pots pitted with imaged wheat.

You send them casting to a deeper source,
A death they do not want to measure. Soon
It will be well they too should learn to bury
The private welter in the public work.

Lead

I stood in Luttrell's Glen. Ash saplings tossed
And Zephyr sullenly came, churning the dust.
A path let in, out of the clash of the light,
Ferns shivering towards a stream. Broken, as slight
As flesh, weak with leaves,
Stone arches bedded in the slope; disused
Forges withered, half in sight,
Their cold lids clumsily slammed; moss on smashed eaves.

I picked from crowded ferns' rooted disorder
Two dull dice of lead. When time blew harder
Vulcan knew them blazing in a heap.
Each weighed so deadly small, feigning a shape;
Both blind, masked as flint,
Stared from the uninhabitable, further
Than clanking furnace, far as the leap
Of first purpose or first accident.

Flame-breathing Vulcan in a maker's rage
Smelted and hammered on his smoking ledge
A bit to bridle Chaos. Hoof by hoof
The red smith snared and shod. Life reared its roof
Over the brilliant back.
Space locked a door. Time set a rock on edge.
I held a stallion's eyes, a stuff
That glared so wild its elements went black.

Drowned in a leafy dusk, paused over metal,
The mind leaped towards the clash of the real.
Its leather-vizored workmen, stuped in flame
And stumbling about such forges, in their time
Roofed many a teeming manor
With sheeted calms no violence could dispel;
Now stood as the light encircled them
Blinded against their black-and-ruddy banner;

Then plunged into the columned Autumn burning.
Craft and craftsman, risen out of nothing,
Sank to a jackdaw chatter in the head.
The road to Dublin churned back into mud.
Gaea, naked as slate,
Caught in her fern those quenched eyes, scarred with seeing
Let drop like dice the aproned dead
Stretched in silence under this estate.

Thinking of Mr D.

A man still light of foot, but ageing, took
An hour to drink his glass, his quiet tongue
Danced to such cheerful slander.

He sipped and swallowed with a scathing smile,
Tapping a polished toe.
His sober nod withheld assent.

When he died I saw him twice.
Once as he used retire
On one last murmured stabbing little tale
From the right company, tucking in his scarf.

And once down by the river, under wharf-
Lamps that plunged him in and out of light,
A priestlike figure turning, wolfish-slim,
Quickly aside from pain, in a bodily plight,
To note the oiled reflections chime and swim.

MORALITIES (1960)

Moralities

Bronze entrance doors alive with angels' wings
Mellow the Western face—a field of stone
Furrowed with devils. Saints in martyred rings
Halo vast windows, light as thistledown.
The wagon empties and a hooting clown
Skips up the shallow steps: 'Ho! Feast your eyes!'
Flounced, scalloped, stuffed with hay, gay skin and bone,
Faith, Love, Death, Song, creep after him like flies.

Faith

An Old Atheist Pauses by the Sea

I choose at random, knowing less and less.
The shambles of the seashore at my feet
Yield a weathered spiral: I confess
—Appalled at how the waves have polished it—
I know that shores are eaten, rocks are split,
Shells ghosted. Something hates unevenness.
The skin turns porcelain, the nerves retreat,
And then the will, and then the consciousness.

Into Thy Hands

Diver, noting lightly how the board
Gives to the body, now with like intent
I watch the body give to the instant, seeing
In risk a salty joy: let accident
Complete our dreadful journey into being.

Here possessed of time and flesh at last,
I hurl the Present bodily at the Past.

Outstretched, into the azure chasm he soared.

A Pillar of the Community

Descending on Merchants' Alley, Lucifer
Gave jet-black evidence of fatherhood.
A column rose to meet him from the mud;
He perched and turned to metal. Polished, foursquare,
A noble savage stopped in stride, he stood.
Now gingerly our honest deals are done
Under that puckish rump, inscribed: Do good.
Some care and a simple faith will get you on.

Love

Seventeenth Century Landscape: near Ballyferriter

A last short-cut along Croaghmarhin's base
Before the dark, the set sun at my back;
On shales of desolation ends my race.

High in the dusk a white horse and a black,
Freed on their separate slopes till morning, pose
A tiny emblematic problem. I ride
—The Three Sisters looming—for the throes
Of rock and water round my castled bride.

Sisters

Grim Deirdre sought the stony fist, her grief
Capped at last by insult. Pierce's bride,
Sybil Ferriter, fluttered like a leaf
And fell in courtly love to stain the tide.
Each for a murdered husband—hanged in silk
Or speared in harness—threw her body wide,
And offered treachery a bloody milk.
Each cast the other's shadow when she died.

A Garden on the Point

Now it is Easter and the speckled bean
Breaks open underground, the liquid snail
Winces and waits, trapped on the lawn's light green;
The burdened clothes-line heaves and barks in the gale,
And lost in flowers near the garage wall
Child and mother fumble, tidy, restrain.

And now great ebb tides lift to the light of day
The sea-bed's briny chambers of decay.

Interlude: Time's Mischief

Love's doubts enrich my words; I stroke them out.
To each felicity, once. He must progress
Who fabricates a path, though all about
Death, Woman, Spring, repeat their first success.

Death

The Doldrums

Two months of blood-summer were in store,
Of strike and rising temper, and the thick sun
A sore that never healed; two months more.
Exhaustion settled over sea and land.

We ushered in midnight at Sutton station,
With the towels damp and sandy, loose in the hand.
Our train clove the serene stars with a roar
In peace and power, on the moment planned.

Sons of the Brave

The great shocked art, the gross great enmity,
That roamed here once, and swept indoors, embalmed
Their lesson with themselves. We shade the eye;
Our mouths have never filled with blood; the shot,
The sung, entwine their ghosts and fade. The sty
They rooted in retains its savour but
Their farrow doze against a Nightmare slammed
Shut in their faces by the prating damned.

Dead on Arrival

It smelled our laughter, then, in vivid shroud,
Loomed with averted face (*Dont think, dont think*),
Limped with its poison through the noisy crowd
And chose my glass. It moaned and begged me: 'Drink.'

I woke in mortal terror, every vein
A-flood with my destroyer; then fought free.
I lie in darkness, treasuring in my brain
The full infection, Night's carnality.

Song

Handclasp at Euston

The engine screams and Murphy, isolate
—Chalk-white, comedian—in the smoky glare,
Dwindles among the churns and tenders. Weight,
Person, race, the human, dwindle there.
I bow to the cases cluttering the rack,
Their handles black with sweat of exile. Wales,
Wave and home; I close my eyes. The track
Swerves to a greener world: sea-rock, thigh-scales.

At the Heart

Heraldic, hatched in gold, a sacred tree
Stands absorbed, tinkering with the slight
Thrumming of birds, the flicker of energy
Thrown and caught, the blows and burdens of flight.
Roots deepen; disciplines proliferate
And wings more fragile are brought into play.
Timber matures, the game grows nobler, yet
Not one has sped direct as appetite.

Fire and Ice

Two creatures face each other, fixed in song,
Satyr and nymph, across the darkening brain.
I dream of reason and the first grows strong,
Drunk as a whirlwind on the sweating grain.
I dream of drunkenness and, freed from strain,
The second murmurs like a fingered gong.
I sink beneath the dream: his words grow sane,
Her pupils glow with pleasure all night long.

DOWNSTREAM (1962)

I wonder whether one expects
Flowing tie or expert sex
Or even absent-mindedness
Of poets any longer. Less
Candour than the average,
Less confidence, a ready rage,
Alertness when it comes to beer,
An affectation that their ear
For music is a little weak,
These are the attributes we seek;
But surely not the morning train,
The office lunch, the look of pain
Down the blotched suburban grass,
Not the weekly trance at Mass . . .
Drawing on my sober dress
These, alas, I must confess.

I pat my wallet pocket, thinking
I can spare an evening drinking;
Humming as I catch the bus
Something by Sibelius,
Suddenly—or as I lend
A hand about the house, or bend
Low above an onion bed—
Memory stumbles in the head;
The sunlight flickers once upon
The massive shafts of Babylon
And ragged phrases in a flock
Settle softly, shock by shock.

And so my bored menagerie
Once more emerges: Energy,
Blinking, only half awake,
Gives its tiny frame a shake;

Fouling itself, a giantess,
The bloodshot bulk of Laziness
Obscures the vision; Discipline
Limps after them with jutting chin,
Bleeding badly from the calf:
Old Jaws-of-Death gives laugh for laugh
With Error as they amble past,
And there as usual, lying last,
Helped along by blind Routine,
Futility flogs a tambourine . . .

1

The Laundress

Her chair drawn to the door,
A basket at her feet,
She sat against the sun
And stitched a linen sheet.
Over harrowed Flanders
August moved the wheat.

Poplars sharing the wind
With Saxony and France
Dreamed at her gate,
Soared in a Summer trance.
A cluck in the cobbled yard:
A shadow changed its stance.

As a fish disturbs the pond
And sinks without a stain
The heels of ripeness fluttered
Under her apron. Then
Her heart grew strained and light
As the shell that shields the grain.

Bluntly through the doorway
She stared at shed and farm,
At yellow fields unstitching
About the hoarded germ,
At land that would spread white
When she had reached her term.

The sower plumps his acre,
Flanders turns to the heat,
The winds of Heaven winnow
And the wheels grind the wheat.
She searched in her basket
And fixed her ruffled sheet.

Wedding Morning

Down the church gravel where the bridal car
    Gleams at the gate among the waifs and strays
And women of Milewater, formal wear
    And Fashion's joker hats wink in the breeze.

Past, the hushed progress under sprays of broom
    And choirs of altar lilies, when all eyes
Went brimming with her and the white-lipped groom
    Brought her to kneel beside him. Past, the sighs;

Ahead lies the gaiety of her father's hall
    Thrown open to the chatter of champagne,
The poised photographer, the flying veil,
    The motors crowded on the squandered lawn.

Down the bright gravel stroll the families
    With Blood, the trader, profiting in their peace.

A Portrait of the Engineer

The frock coat and the snowy cuff
Sit well; he handles a bright black hat;
Lips that a moderate span of life
Tautened and drew down are shut.
The boardroom sun dwells on the glass-
And-gold gleam of his picture frame.

Monuments to storm and stress
Endure in foreign lands; at home
Girders lift the lower sky,
Ramps and funnels thunder, all
Born of a dour intensity
That cramped and frowned and drove until
His earthly visions turned to stone
And complex Profit dammed his passion.
Power leaped from son to son
And gathered calm in their succession;

34

All throve with honour, none fell short
Or raised the fingers to the mouth
When change demanded they take part
In humanism's privy death
To keep that calm unbroken. Now,
To a later eye, the paint reveals
That full logic, plain to see
Alert in his steely spectacles.

And there in a calm within a calm,
Spotless on the heavy baize,
His instrument, a diagram,
Is set to wither mysteries.

Full-fed upon the hushed, glass-smooth
Absorption of its master's desk
A demon rose from the finished task,
Drew intoxicated breath
And flexed its golden strength to pester
The lazy places of the earth.

But when did demon usher master
Lightly from the toils of birth?
On marsh and moor his mind was bent
Till slowly they gave up their hearts
And split the seam of his content.

Another of the brutal arts
Feeds a second demon where
(Ambiguous sympathy gone dumb)
I knock my shoe against a chair
And turn toward sunlight. If it should come
To pass at length that our ghosts met
We'd match our questions in a gaze:
Mine for the flesh his engines ate,
His for the blurred response of a phrase.

Charlie

It shuffled round and round a concrete log,
Swung on a bar, dropped to the smelly boards,
Weaved on worn-out knuckles into a corner,
Sat in a nest of straw and scratched an armpit.

I thought of Jacob on his midden mourning
For strayed and straying sons. And then its neck,
Weary and slack with prison, came erect
And Jacob's glittering eye peered out upon us.

A sudden trick of shadow gave its face
A look of chill yet fatherly concern;
It raised a thick grave paw, the fingers toward us,
And gestured all to settle on the straw.

'Come from the light of the sun,' it seemed to say,
'Into the mindless dusk, and we'll repeat
The open vowels of our common Fathers
Forever. Come to my dandruff paradise.'

Scylla and Charybdis

Abstracted, sour, as he reaches across a dish
Of plaice, his hand on a tray of birds, O'Neill
Unplugs the weary fan: flat heaps of fish
Exhale. He watches Reynolds grope and pile
His window opposite with melons, fresh
Leather of cabbage, oranges . . . and smile.

Wiping his gamy hands he turns and thirsts
Abruptly for clay and fragrance, until it seems
The South in a sweet globe sinks to his lips and bursts.
And yet red-wristed Reynolds dreams and dreams
That he flies with the snipe in the sparse bracken, or thrusts
Cold muscle to the depths and dumbly screams.

I have slipped at evening through that ghostly quarrel,
Making a third, to round the simple moral.

Dick King

In your ghost, Dick King, in your phantom vowels I read
That death roves our memories igniting
Love. Kind plague, low voice in a stubbled throat,
You haunt with the taint of age and of vanished good,
Fouling my thought with losses.

Clearly now I remember rain on the cobbles,
Ripples in the iron trough, and the horses' dipped
Faces under the Fountain in James's Street,
When I sheltered my nine years against your buttons
And your own dread years were to come:

And your voice, in a pause of softness, named the dead,
Hushed as though the city had died by fire,
Bemused, discovering . . . discovering
A gate to enter temperate ghosthood by;
And I squeezed your fingers till you found again
My hand hidden in yours.

                              I squeeze your fingers:

            Dick King was an upright man.
            Sixty years he trod
            The dull stations underfoot.
            Fifteen he lies with God.

            By the salt seaboard he grew up
            But left its rock and rain
            To bring a dying language east
            And dwell in Basin Lane.

            By the Southern Railway he increased:
            His second soul was born
            In the clangour of the iron sheds,
            The hush of the late horn.

An invalid he took to wife.
She prayed her life away;
Her whisper filled the whitewashed yard
Until her dying day.

And season in, season out,
He made his wintry bed.
He took the path to the turnstile
Morning and night till he was dead.

He clasped his hands in a Union ward
To hear St James's bell.
I searched his eyes though I was young,
The last to wish him well.

Cover Her Face

She has died suddenly, aged twenty-nine years, in Dublin. Some of her family travel from the country to bring her body home. Having driven all morning through a storm

1

They dither softly at her bedroom door
In soaking overcoats, and words forsake
Even their comforters. The bass of prayer
Haunts the chilly landing while they take
Their places in a murmur of heartbreak.

Shabby with sudden tears, they know their part,
Mother and brother, resigning all that ends
At these drab walls. For here, with panicked heart,
A virgin broke the seal; who understands
The sheet pulled white and Maura's locked blue hands?

Later her frown will melt, when by degrees
They flinch from grief. A girl they have never seen,
Sunk now in love and horror to her knees,
The black official giving discipline
To shapeless sorrow, these are more their kin,

38

By grace of breath, than that grave derelict
Whose blood and feature, like a sleepy host,
Agreed a while with theirs. Her body's tact
Swapped child for woman, woman for a ghost,
Until its buried sleep lay uppermost;

And Maura, come to terms at last with pain,
Rests in her ruptured mind, her temples tight,
Patiently weightless as her time burns down.
Soon her few glories will be shut from sight:
Her slightness, the fine metal of her hair spread out,

Her cracked, sweet laugh. Such gossamers as hold
Friends, family—all fortuitous conjunction—
Sever with bitter whispers; with untold
Peace shrivel to their anchors in extinction.
There, newly trembling, others grope for function.

2

Standing by the door, effaced in self,
I cannot deny her death, protest, nor grieve,
Dogged by a scrap of memory: some tossed shelf
Holds, a secret shared, that photograph,
Her arm tucked tiredly into mine; her laugh,

As though she also knew a single day
Would serve to bleed us to a diagram,
Sighs and confides. She waived validity
The night she drank the furnace of the Lamb,
Draining one image of its faint *I am*.

I watch her drift, in doubt whether dead or born
—Not with Ophelia's strewn virginity
But with a pale unmarriage—out of the worn
Bulk of day, under its sightless eye,
And close her dream in hunger. So we die.

Monday, without regret, darkens the pane
And sheds on the shaded living, the crystal soul,
A gloomy lustre of the pouring rain.
Nuns have prepared her for the holy soil
And round her bed the faded roses peel

That the fruit of justice may be sown in peace
To them that make peace, and bite its ashen bread.
Mother, brother, when our questions cease
Such peace may come, consenting to the good,
Chaste, biddable, out of all likelihood.

Girl on a Swing

My touch has little force:
Her infant body falls.
Her lips lightly purse
With panic and delight
And fly up to kiss
The years' brimming glass;
To drink; to sag sweetly
When I drop from sight.

Navigators

The swivelled lantern flares, shears
A granite staircase wet from the pier's
Flank and fingers over a strewn
Breakwater in the fog, to drown
Its long beam where the night mows down.

Two shrouded lovers come for whom
Lamps on the concrete sea-wall bloom
And adamant levels under the Head
—Cold contrivances of the dead
Protectors of harbours—spring to the tread.

When these unlink and sigh and sleep
Aphrodite'll walk the deep.
Weaving a garland she will break
A cry from either soul and pluck
The shore-bird's psychotic shriek.

So navigators under threat
Of their extinction overset
The harsh horn and the hollow bell
Against the reef, against the swell,
Ephemeral, perpetual.

2

Check

A naked foot steps out onto bare baked mud.

Blue-and-scarlet live crystals of gossamer,
Burning giant dragonflies, hum and vanish,
Glass-dreams shimmering above outermost reeds.

The coppery lake lies calm, heavy lidded.
A yawning phantom scythes the brackish water
Then backs again under a stone overhang.

A plain, a vast horizon, a quiet beast,
Awaiting the lifting up of human eyes.

Tyrant Dying

Fat hands, no longer guided, rest their talons,
The bone- and sinew-shattering pen let fall.
His wasted legs lie cauterised to rest.

Bloodstained content, madness of dusk-at-noon,
Heart's petrifaction, these have been merciful.
Time's vacant mercy gathers now at his head,
Time for his holy death, as the schoolbooks tell,
Kisskissing his servants' hands in agony.

Blank eyes turn toward Heaven. The pain-dark face
—Skewed like a night-cap on his mighty body—
Glistens in the bedroom's single yellow ray,
Where angels descending and in pain ascending
Bring him peace, searing memory to the root.

Deeds long accomplished with an amputating
Acid violence, steeled against revulsion,

Fly up with sighs of gratitude and away,
And speechless now above death's mirroring parchment
Pale, tilted heads toss slowly, blotting it red.

Blind eyes turn inward: through the withering shades
Peace awaits him, dark as a propped axe.

Old Harry

Death states the theme

'Master Love', my grim instructor assured me,
'Moved already in the criminal darkness
Before our dust was chosen, or choice began,

Devising—for spirits that would not fall asunder
At a touch—a flesh of thirst and pain, a blood
Driven by onward self-torment and by desire.'

'*What of the guilty spirit*', I inquired,
'*Inviting darkness to the human womb?*'
'The guilty will repay with flesh and blood.'

'*What of the innocent spirit, in pursuit
Of justice and the good?*' 'The innocent
Repay with flesh and blood.' Then we proceeded.

The Twilight of Old Harry

Pink eyelids dipped in terror. Softly, possessed,
Voles flew like shuttles through the brush. A buzzard
Completed its loop of threat above the trees.

He marched with feeble vigour through the forest.
Down dappled levels of oak, alleys of beech,
Beams of sunlight flickered on his hide of tweed

And flared on his spectacles, two sightless coins.
In a quiet clearing, round a turn of the path,
He laid on a rich red tree his mottled hand

43

Who time and time again brought it down sharply
To put a stop, when he had cause, to anger,
The dangers of narrow thought, or mere habit,

How many years ago . . . Like steel children
Around his gleaming table they advised
And were absorbed, as he imposed reason

—A curb to the rash, a pupil to the wise.
Until on a certain day he waved them out,
Thoughtful before his maps. And chose at last

The greater terror for the lesser number.
With rounded cheeks he blew a moral blast
And the two chosen cities of the plain

Lost their flesh and blood—tiles, underwear, wild cries
Stripped away in gales of light. Lascivious streets
Heightened their rouge and welcomed baths of pure flame.

In broad daylight delicate creatures of love
Opened their thighs. Their breasts melted shyly
And bared the white bone. At that sight

Men blushed fiercely and became shades.
The air in a passion inhaled, and all dissolved
Or collapsed shimmering on black recesses,

A silken scenery of Heaven and Hell;
Exhaled, and the tympanum of earth shuddered,
Day cracked like a lantern and its blazing oils

Soared up in turmoil in thick vessels of dust.
Anthropophagi moaned in the buckling cloud,
Amazons and chimaerae, leaving the world.

Where once the cities of wickedness had stood
Eye sockets with nerves and ducts smouldering,
Moistened like two wells the plain's enamelled face.

A scrap of autumn silence came fluttering down
To touch his wrist with its invisible lace.
He shivered in golden light.

                       The scabby trunk
Broke the surface of his dream. He scratched
In vacant memory of mucous pleasure.

A nest of twittering naked animals.
Eyes clenched, grinning together in blind terror,
They tremble snout to snout, appearing to kiss.

A paw strokes a soft flank as though to comfort.
At each light touch a little blood enriches
The threads linking heart to heart and lip to lip.

A Country Walk

Sick of the piercing company of women,
I swung the gate shut with a furious sigh,
Rammed trembling hands in pockets and drew in
A breath of river air.
                    A rook's wet wing
Cuffed abruptly upward through the drizzle.

On either hand, dead trunks in drapes of creeper.
I walked their hushed stations, passion dying,
Each slow footfall a drop of peace returning.

I clapped my gloves. Three cattle turned aside
Their fragrant bodies from a corner gate,
Churning land to liquid in their passage.
Briefly through the beaded grass a path
Led to the holy stillness of a well,
And there in the smell of water, stone and leaf
I knelt, baring my hand, and scooped and drank.

And soon proceeded with a lighter step.
Down the river valley, wide and quiet,

An aqueduct—cat-backed, in delicate ruin—
Rooted to one horizon. On the other
A great asylum reared its potent calm.

A steeple; the long yielding of a railway turn
Through thorn and willow. Joining the two slopes,
Blocking an ancient way with barracks and brewery,
A town received the river. Lines of roofs
Fused in veils of mist and steely light.
A strand of idle smoke mounted until
An idler current combed it slowly West,
A hook of shadow dividing the still sky.

I passed a marshy field: that shallow ford
A place of bloodshed, as the tales agree.
There, the day that Christ hung dying, twin
Brothers armed in hate; the day darkened;
They crossed swords under a full eclipse
And mingled their bowels at the saga's end.
There the first Normans massacred my fathers
Then stroked their armoured horses' necks, disposed
In ceremony, sable on green sward.
Twice more the reeds grew red: when knot-necked Cromwell
Despatched a convent shrieking to their Lover;
And when a rebel host, through long retreat
Grown half hysterical—methodical, ludicrous—
Piked Cromwell's puritan brood, their harmless neighbours,
Into the sharp water in groups of three,
Then melted into the martyred countryside,
Root eaters, strange as badgers.

Road and river parted and my path
Entered the town. I passed a concrete cross
Low in the ditch; for one who answered latest
The phantom hag.
                    There he bled to death,
His line of sight blocked by the corner stone,
And never saw the streets ablaze with joy,
The grinning foe driven from the field
In heavy lorries. And his mortal meat

Was whole still in the Hill Cemetery
When freedom burned his comrades' itchy palms,
Too much for flesh and blood and, armed in hate,
Brother met brother in a modern light.

They turned the final corner, knelt and killed,
Who gather still at Easter round his grave,
Our watchful elders. Mixed among his bones
He takes their soil, and chatting they return
To take their town again, that have exchanged
A trenchcoat playground for a gombeen jungle.

Around the corner, on the Market Square,
I came upon the sombre monuments
That bear their names: MacDonagh and McBride,
Merchants; Connolly's Commercial Arms . . .
I walked their shopfronts, the declining light
Playing on lens and raincoat stonily,
And turned away.

                    Across the open ground
A lamp switched on above the urinal.
Over the silent handball alley, eyes
That never looked on lover measured mine
Over the Christian Brothers' frosted glass
And turned sway.

                    Out of the neighbouring shades
A car plunged soundlessly and disappeared
Across the bridge. A naked sycamore
Dripping near the corner of the quay
Let fall from its combining arms a single
Word on my upturned face.

                         The parapet
Above the central arch received my hands.

Under a darkening and clearing heaven
The hastening river flowed in a slate sheen,
Its face a-swarm. A thousand currents broke,
Kissing, dismembering, in threads of foam
Or poured intact over the stony bed
Glass-green and chill. Their shallow, shifting waters

Slid on in troubled union, mixing together
Surfaces that gave and swallowed light.
And grimly the flood divided where it swept
An endless debris through the failing dusk
Under the trembling span beneath my feet.

Venit Hesperus.
In green and golden light.
                                    Bringing sweet trade.

Downstream

We gave our frail craft to the slow-moving stream,
Ruffling the waters, and steadied on a seam
Of calm and current. Together, both as one,
We thrust ourselves forward, thrusting behind
Old willows with their shadows half undone
And groves of alder mowing like the blind
In the last light. A swan in muffled stress,
Disturbed, flew off downstream. Ghost of whiteness.

We drifted onward in encircling silence,
Talking of poetry. I read a page
Out of the Cantos, and the scroll of names
Ascended in the half light, silken kings
Luminous with crisis.
                        I closed the book,
The gathering shades beginning to deceive,
And wiped the dewy cover on my sleeve.

*

We halted by a thorn, under the bank
Of a tributary stream. He clambered out,
I held on by a branch.
                        Night whispering;
The lips of liquid.
                        And I took my turn
Naming old signs above the Central Plain.
Distant light replied, a word of thunder.

*

We stabbed at the water. Toward the woods of Durrow.

A ghost of white on the blackvelvet face
Fluttered and quietened, serenely gliding;
Sipping at the darkness and receding.

Thick slopes from shore to shore
Lowered a matted arch and moved out roots,
Full of slant pike, over the river floor.

The black cage closed about us:
                              furred night-brutes
Stopped and listened, twitching their tiny brushes.

Then I remembered how, among those bushes,
A man one night fell sick and left his shell
Collapsed, half eaten, like a rotted thrush's

To frighten stumbling children. 'You could tell',
My co-shadow murmured, 'by the hands
He died in trouble.' And the cold of hell,

A limb-lightness, a terror in the glands,
Pierced again as when that story first
Stopped my blood. The soil of other lands

Drank lives that summer with a body thirst.
Nerveless by the European pit,
Ourselves through seven hundred years accurst,

We saw the barren world obscurely lit
By tall chimneys flickering in their pall,
The haunt of swinish man. Each day a spit

That, turning, sweated war. Each night a fall
Back to the evil dream where rodents ply,
Man-rumped, sow-headed, busy with whip and maul

Among nude herds of the damned. It seemed that I,
Coming to conscience on that edge of dread,
Still dreamed, impervious to calamity,

Imagining a formal drift of the dead
Stretched calm as effigies on velvet dust,
Scattered on starlit slopes with arms outspread

And eyes of silver . . . When that story thrust
Pungent horror and an actual mess
Into my very face, and taste I must.

*

Like mortal jaws, the alleys of the wood
Fell-to behind us. At their heart, a ghost
That glimmered briefly with my gift of blood,

Spreadeagled on a rack of leaves, almost
Remembering, facing the crowded sky,
Calmly encountering the starry host,

Meeting their silver eyes with silver eye,
An X of wavering flesh, a skull of light,
Fading in our wake without a sigh.

*

Soon the current shuddered in its flight,
Swerving on pliant muscle. We were sped
Through sudden peace into a pit of night

—The Mill Hole, whose rocky fathoms fed
On moss and pure depth and the cold fin
Turning in its heart. The river bed

Called to our flesh from under the watery skin.
Breathless, our shell trembled across the abyss;
I held my oar in fear. When deeper in

Something shifted in sleep, a quiet hiss
At peace, as we slipped past. A milk-white breast,
A shift of wings, betraying with feathery kiss

A soul of white with darkness for a nest.
The creature bore the night so tranquilly
I lifted up my eyes. There without rest

The phantoms of the overhanging sky
Occupied their stations and descended.
Another moment, to the starlit eye,

The slow, downstreaming dead, it seemed, were blended
One with those silver hordes, and briefly shared
Their order, glittering. And then impended

A barrier of rock that turned and bared
A varied barrenness as toward its base
We glided—blotting heaven as it towered—

Searching the darkness for a landing place.

3

Chrysalides

Our last free summer we mooned about at odd hours
Pedalling slowly through country towns, stopping to eat
Chocolate and fruit, tracing our vagaries on the map.

At night we watched in the barn, to the lurch of melodeon music,
The crunching boots of countrymen—huge and weightless
As their shadows—twirling and leaping over the yellow concrete.

Sleeping too little or too much, we awoke at noon
And were received with womanly mockery into the kitchen,
Like calves poking our faces in with enormous hunger.

Daily we strapped our saddlebags and went to experience
A tolerance we shall never know again, confusing
For the last time, for example, the licit and the familiar.

Our instincts blurred with change; a strange wakefulness
Sapped our energies and dulled our slow-beating hearts
To the extremes of feeling—insensitive alike

To the unique succession of our youthful midnights,
When by a window ablaze softly with the virgin moon
Dry scones and jugs of milk awaited us in the dark,

Or to lasting horror: a wedding flight of ants
Spawning to its death, a mute perspiration
Glistening like drops of copper, agonised, in our path.

String Puppets

At his desk, lonely, Richard, his tie loose
About his throat, his hands loose at his sides.
His white face jerks up to the chalk light.

Lamplit by the hell-dark laurel hedge
There stood erect in soiled evening dress
One sombrely displaying a starched breast,
Lionlike hair agleam on a dried skull;
Lifting, with a deadly exhaling smile,
Claws outstretched up to the lighted window.

Exit Richard, dying. Manipulated
On withering cords, his high shoulders hooked
To an infinitely proceeding Heaven.

Brothers

I have come with wingéd step, stick in hand, hound at heel,
Over high ridges of rock, through tempest of salt and sun
And pounding wind, prevailing from end to end upon
The island heights.

The dog, catching at breath with tongue and maddened ribs,
Paws a slant stone, carved against oceanic cloud,
Against crumpled mainland peaks diminished by a void
Seven miles of water.

A blaze of my pity consumes his gasping eagerness
Islanded in storm, his coat shivering-on-end.
A flayed image, ridged and trembling, is laid bare
And its flesh is glass:

A model of sinews, fragile tissue and channelled blood,
Of live translucencies crimson in the driving gale,
To horrify and instruct. In the spasm of Sentience
Beast and man are made one.

The Force of Eloquence

Unbrooding as an ox, he thrusts a bald
Muscular head out smiling. Into his tongue
Chains are fastened, radii of bronze.
Firmly held by these, his swayed captives
Yield their wrists against a line of hills.

Equilibrium of gift and threat;
Of speech constricted into other terms,
Moulded in eternal breathless appearance.

Enter and inhale the living bronze.

Mirror in February

The day dawns with scent of must and rain,
Of opened soil, dark trees, dry bedroom air.
Under the fading lamp, half dressed—my brain
Idling on some compulsive fantasy—
I towel my shaven jaw and stop, and stare,
Riveted by a dark exhausted eye,
A dry downturning mouth.

It seems again that it is time to learn,
In this untiring, crumbling place of growth
To which, for the time being, I return.
Now plainly in the mirror of my soul
I read that I have looked my last on youth
And little more; for they are not made whole
That reach the age of Christ.

Below my window the awakening trees,
Hacked clean for better bearing, stand defaced
Suffering their brute necessities,
And how should the flesh not quail that span for span
Is mutilated more? In slow distaste
I fold my towel with what grace I can,
Not young and not renewable, but man.

NIGHTWALKER AND OTHER POEMS (1968)

Our Mother

Tall windows full of sea light,
Two women and a child in tears
Silent among screens and flowers,
The ward a quiet zone of air.

The girl whimpers in bed, remote
Under the anaesthetic still.
She sleeps on her new knowledge, a bride
With bowels burning and disarrayed.

She dreams a red Gorgon-mask
Warped in the steel kidney dish,
The tender offals of her core
Worming around the raw stare.

Her mother watches, struck dumb.
Tears of recognition run
For the stranger, daughter, self, on whom
In fascination her eyes feed,

As mine on her—a revenant,
A rain-worn, delicate
Stone shape that has looked long
Into that other face direct.

In the next bed, dying of age,
The carrier of all our harm
Turns on us an emptiness
Of open mouth and damp eyes.

All three women, two in my care,
The third beyond all care, in tears.
Living, dying, I meet their stare
Everywhere, and cannot move.

Office for the Dead

The grief-chewers enter, their shoes hard on the marble,
In white lace and black skirts, books held to their loins.
A silver pot tosses in its chains as they assemble
About the coffin, heavy under its cloth, and begin.

Back and forth, each side in nasal unison
Against the other, their voices grind across her body.
We watch, kneeling like children, and shrink as their Church
Latin chews our different losses into one

—All but certain images of her pain that will not,
In the coarse process, pass through the cloth and hidden boards
To their peace in the shroud; that delay, still real—

High thin shoulders—eyes boring out of the dusk—
Wistful misshapenness—a stripped, dazzling mouth—
Her frown as she takes the candle pushed into her hands
In the last crisis, propped up, dying with worry.

Sanctus. We listen with bowed heads to the thrash of chains
Measuring the silence. The pot gasps in its smoke.
An animal of metal, dragging itself and breathing.

Ballydavid Pier

Noon. The luminous tide
Climbs through the heat, covering
Grey shingle. A film of scum
Searches first among litter,
Cloudy with (I remember)
Life; then crystal-clear shallows
Cool on the stones, silent
With shells and claws, white fish bones;
Farther out a bag of flesh,
Foetus of goat or sheep,
Wavers below the surface.

Allegory forms of itself:
The line of life creeps upward
Replacing one world with another,
The welter of its advance
Sinks down into clarity,
Slowly the more foul
Monsters of loss digest.

Small monster of true flesh
Brought forth somewhere
In bloody confusion and error
And flung into bitterness,
Blood washed white:
Does that structure satisfy?

The ghost tissue hangs unresisting
In allegorical waters,
Lost in self-search
—A swollen blind brow
Humbly crumpled over
Budding limbs, unshaken
By the spasms of birth or death.

The Angelus. Faint bell-notes
From some church in the distance
Tremble over the water.
It is nothing. The vacant harbour
Is filling; it will empty.
The misbirth touches the surface
And glistens like quicksilver.

Landscape and Figure

A man stoops low on the overcast plain. He is earthing
Or uprooting among heavy leaves. In the whole field
One dull poppy burns, on the drill by his boots.

The furrows yield themselves to his care. He does not
Lift his head; and would not, though the blight
Breathed on his fields out of the low clouds.

The blight breathes, or does not, invisibly,
As it will. Stalks still break into scattered flower.
Tissue forms about purpose as about seed.

He works toward the fruit of Adam. It darkens the plain,
Its seed a huge brain. The protecting flesh
When it falls will melt away in a kind of mud.

Museum

Out of doors the season dies, a fountain
Ruffles in the wind. The great Museum
Squats closer on its hoard and will not move.
Its blocks of granite, speechless with fatigue,
Imply the slithering pit, the shapelessly-
Adjusting matter of the rubbish heap.

Webs of corridors and numbered rooms
Catch the onward turbulence of forms
Against museum technique; the flux disperses
In order everywhere, in glass cases
Or draped or towering in enormous gloom.
Human voice and footstep die.

A dozen tiny coarse clay animals
Picked from a midden—hook-winged geese or hawks,
A bull with pitted head free to move—
Squat blindly. The remote curator speaks:
'In the beginning there were toys, implying love.'
Voice and footstep die away.

A Moment's Peace

Summer evening: reclining
Lovers, a pike near the bank,
Stone-still—carnivores,
Ephemerides, touched with gold.
The river surface flows
On in blank passion.

Traveller

Behind me my children vanish, left asleep
In their strange bed, in apple-tasted night.
I drive from worry to worry, to where my wife
Struggles for her breath in a private room.

An hour to midnight, and the traps of self
Are open for eighty solitary miles ahead,
In the swerving ditch, in the flash of tree-trunks and hedges.

The brain, woken to itself and restless,
Senses their black mouths muttering in the darkness:
Phrases, echoes of feeling, from other journeys
To bait and confuse the predatory will
And draw it aside, muttering in absent response,
Down stale paths in the dark to a stale lair,
In brainless trance, where it can treadle and chew
Old pangs blunter and smoother, old self-mutilations.

Far ahead on the road the lamps caught something.
A cat. A bird. Mesmerised. It moved,
Eating. It rose slowly, white furred, and flew
Up into the dark. An owl! My heart
Stood still. I had forgotten the very existence . . .

Westland Row

We came to the outer light down a ramp in the dark
Through eddying cold gusts and grit, our ears
Stopped with noise. The hands of the station clock
Stopped, or another day vanished exactly.
The engine departing hammered slowly overhead.
Dust blowing under the bridge, we stooped slightly
With briefcases and books and entered the wind.

The savour of our days restored, dead
On nostril and tongue. Drowned in air,
We stepped on our own traces, not on stone,
Nodded and smiled distantly and followed
Our scattering paths, not stumbling, not touching.

Until, in a breath of benzine from a garage-mouth,
By the Academy of Music coming against us
She stopped an instant in her wrinkled coat
And ducked her childish cheek in the coat-collar
To light a cigarette: seeing nothing,
Thick-lipped, in her grim composure.

Daughterwife, look upon me.

Folk Wisdom

Each year for a short season
The toads stare and wait
And clutch in their being
A shrieking without breath.
There is nothing but the harrow—
Everything speaks its approach;
Even blades of grass,
Flower stems, are harrows' teeth,
Hideous, because they are
Parallel and in earth.

The men are shackling their horses
In the yard. They talk softly
About earth and seed.

Soon the toads will shriek—
Each, as he hears his neighbour,
Gathers all his strength.

And so the curse was lifted,
According to the tale;
One kiss, and a prince stood there
Where a toad had been.

It is possible . . . such a strain,
Under the kiss of the harrow,
Could suffice. As when a man
Clutches his ears, deafened
By his world, to find a jewel
Made of pain in his hands.

Tara

The mist hung on the slope, growing whiter
On the thin grass and dung by the mounds;
It hesitated at the dyke, among briars.

Our children picked up the wrapped flasks, capes and baskets
And we trailed downward among whins and thrones
In a muffled dream, guided by slender axe-shapes.

Our steps scattered on the soft turf, leaving
No trace, the childrens' voices like light.
Low in the sky behind us, a vast silver shield

Seethed and consumed itself in the thick ether.
A horse appeared at the rampart like a ghost
And tossed his neck at ease, with a hint of harness.

WORMWOOD

and a great star fell from heaven, burning as it were a torch; and it fell on the third part of the rivers and upon the fountains of waters; and the name of the star is called Wormwood; and the third part of the waters became wormwood; and many men died of the waters, because they were made bitter.
—Apocalypse: Ch. 8, vv. 10 and 11

Beloved,

A little of what we have found.

It is certain that maturity and peace are to be sought through ordeal after ordeal, and it seems that the search continues until we fail. We reach out after each new beginning, penetrating our context to know ourselves, and our knowledge increases until we recognise again (more profoundly each time) our pain, indignity and triviality. This bitter cup is offered, heaped with curses, and we must drink or die. And even though we drink we may also die, if every drop of bitterness—that rots the flesh—is not transmuted. (Certainly the individual plight is hideous, each torturing each, but we are guilty, seeing this, to believe that our common plight is only hideous. Believing so, we make it so: pigs in a slaughteryard that turn and savage each other in a common desperation and disorder.) Death, either way, is guilt and failure. But if we drink bitterness and can transmute it and continue, we resume in candour and doubt the only individual joy—the restored necessity to learn. Sensing a wider scope, a more penetrating harmony, we begin again in a higher innocence to grow toward the next ordeal.

Love also, it seems, will continue until we fail: in the sensing of the wider scope, in the growth toward it, in the swallowing and absorption of bitterness, in the resumed innocence.

Open this and you will see
A waste, a nearly naked tree
That will not rest till it is bare,
But shivers, shivers in the air
Scraping at its yellow leaves.
Winter, when the tempest heaves,
It riots in the heaven-sent
Convulsions of self-punishment.

What cannot rest till it is bare,
Though branches crack and fibres tear?

Wormwood

I have dreamt it again: standing suddenly still
In a thicket, among wet trees, stunned, minutely
Shuddering, hearing a wooden echo escape.

A mossy floor, almost colourless, disappears
In depths of rain among the tree shapes.
I am straining, tasting that echo a second longer.

If I can hold it . . . familiar if I can hold it.
A black tree with a double trunk—two trees
Grown into one—throws up its blurred branches.

The two trunks in their infinitesimal dance of growth
Have turned completely about one another, their join
A slowly twisted scar, that I recognise . . .

A quick arc flashes sidewise in the air,
A heavy blade in flight. A wooden stroke:
Iron sinks in the gasping core.

I will dream it again.

Mask of Love

Mask of Love,
Do you turn to us for peace?
Me, flinching from your stare?
Her, whose face you bear?

Remember how we have climbed
The peaks of stress and stood
Wearily again and again,
Face to face
Across the narrow abyss.

Remember
That our very bodies lack peace:
In tiny darknesses
The skin angrily flames,
Nerve gropes for muscle
Across the silent abyss.

You have seen our nocturnal
Suicidal dance:
She, bent on some tiny mote;
I, doubled in laughter,
Clasping my paunch in grief
For the world in a speck of dust;
Between us, the fuming abyss.

Dumb vapours pour
Where the mask of Love appears,
Reddening, and disappears.

The Secret Garden

The place is growing difficult. Flails of bramble
Crawl into the lawn; on every hand
Glittering, toughened branches drink their dew.
Tiny worlds, drop by drop, tremble
On thorns and leaves; they will melt away.
The silence whispers around us:
Wither, wither, visible, invisible!

A child stands an instant at my knee.
His mouth smells of energy, light as light.
I touch my hand to his pearl flesh, taking strength.
He stands still, absorbing in return
The first taint. Immaculate, the waiting
Kernel of his brain.
How set him free, a son, toward the sour encounter?

Children's voices somewhere call his name.
He runs glittering into the sun, and is gone
. . . I cultivate my garden for the dew:
A rasping boredom funnels into death!
The sun climbs, a creature of one day,
And the dew dries to dust.
My hand strays out and picks off one sick leaf.

First Light

A prone couple still sleeps.
Light ascends like a pale gas
Out of the sea: dawn-light
Reaching across the hill
To the dark garden. The grass
Emerges, soaking with grey dew.

Inside, in silence, an empty
Kitchen takes form, tidied and swept,
Blank with marriage—where shrill
Lover and beloved have kept
Another vigil far
Into the night, and raved and wept.

Upstairs a whimper or sigh
Comes from an open bedroom door
And lengthens to an ugly wail
—A child enduring a dream
That grows, at the first touch of day,
Unendurable.

Remembering Old Wars

What clamped us together? When each night fell we lay down
In the smell of decay and slept, our bodies leaking,
Limp as the dead, breathing that smell all night.

Then light prodded us awake, and adversity
Flooded up from inside us as we laboured upright
Once more to face the hells of circumstance.

And so on, without hope of change or peace.
Each dawn, like lovers recollecting their purpose,
We would renew each other with a savage smile.

Je t'adore

The other props are gone.
Sighing in one another's
Iron arms, propped above nothing,
We praise Love the limiter.

The Shoals Returning
In memory of Gerry Flaherty, drowned 1959

I dip the oar and lean
Supported and opposed
On the green flesh of a wave.
The ocean depth swallows
My strength like a stone.

A corpse, balanced
Among striped fathoms,
Turns over face upward.

He comes from the sea

Down at the gorge mouth
Slow as a floating stick
A light boat is borne
Into the hall of rock.
It edges to a slope of stone
And washes back and forth,
Treading the watery floor.
Faint strokes of the oars
Echo in the chasm.
A man in cap and boots
Throws his coat onto the slip:
He stoops and flings out
The body of a cod,
A sheaf of slithering mackerel,
A handful of crabs' claws.

*

He passes on the cliff road
Against depths of marine light:
Narrow-necked, erect, averse,
In coarse grey jacket and trousers,
Wrists loose, his eyes
Black points of spray.

67

A slow harsh thunder
From below—the Wave of Tóime
Snarls with distance, shudders
In its caves and writhes milkily.
A ragged foam-web joining
And unlinking among the rocks
Seizes the cliff in white turmoil,
Sighs and crumbles,
Breakers against breakers,
Chewing the solid earth.

He sings

A voice rises flickering
From palatal darkness, a thin yell
Straining erect, checked
In glottal silence. The song
Articulates and pierces.

A boot scrapes the floor. Live eyes
Shine, each open on its rock,
In horn-darkness of paraffin,
Rope and gas cylinders.
Wet glasses of stout
Cling to boxes and casks.
Men, sunk in shade,
Listen on their benches,
Bodies tainted with sea wind.
Their eyes respond; squat entities
Turn in cranial darkness
In the ravenous element
At the innermost turn of the shell.

He sings at the back of the shop:
Slit eyes above high cheeks,
Jaws drawn back,
Teeth bared to the voice.
In the exercise of his gift
His throat constricts.

68

Speech, human proportion,
Distort to permit the cry
That can prepare the spirit
To turn softly and be eaten
In the smell of brine and blood.

Dark shell breath, tatters of mist
And sea foam blown from the waves
Fly inland. Soiled feathers
Scatter on the shingle.
Sea birds' fleeting bodies
Pierce the wind.

He returns

That Autumn, after fifteen years,
A new direction
Loosened the seed in the depths.
The mackerel shoals reappeared
And the water in the Sound shivered.
The boats waited at Smerwyck,
Black skinned, crook backed,
On the grass by the drying boat-slip;
The rocky knife-sharp shore
Drained bare: crayfish stared:
Brutal torso of conger
Slid through a choked slit
—Naked savagery
Under a sheet of water
Cut by black blades of rock.
By nightfall the bay ran cold
With the distant returning tide
Under the wall of Mount Brandon,
And the clefts brimmed in darkness.

*

Booted spirits are at work;
A heavy step scrapes on the slip;
A boat tosses with a feathery splash.
They vanish over covered rocks
With crisp tangles of net,
Vague oar-voices,
The taint of canvas and rope,
Past cliff wall and washed rocks
Over meshes of hissing foam.
They cross into the Sound
And climb the swell blindly,
Dropping in dark valleys.

Nets are shaken out
And swallowed into the sea,
The lines reaching far down,
Opening everywhere
Among the haunted levels
Where a million shadows
Pursue their staring will
Along echoing cold paths.
The delicate veil of garottes
Drags, scarcely breathing,
Then touches a living shoal.
Fierce bodies leap into being
Strangling all over the net;
They gather weight, shudder
By shudder—staring about them—
An anguish of shivering lives.

He disappears

Dawn opened on a jewel
Turning in the ocean
Under the empty boat,
A net of suffocated fish
Tied fast to the seat board
Pulling the head down in the waves:

Two thousand mackerel
Torn out of the shoal,
Stopped dead and gathered up
With mourning devils' mouths
And scales and rigid eyes
In a cluster shaped by its own weight
Against the meshes of its bonds.
The drowned men have fallen away
Through the water and separated
With slow hair in the calm;
Their jewel drifting until it rots
To pieces, for anyone to find.

*

A withered man,
A coat across his shoulders,
Watches from the cliff
—A black outcrop thrust
Partly out of the soil
Up into the salt wind.
The shale-grass shivers around him.

He turns a shrunken mask
Of cheekbone and jawbone
And pursed ancient mouth
Out over the sea surface.
His eyes, under tortoise lids,
Assess the crystalline plasm,
Formations of water
Under falls of air.

Before Sleep

It is time for bed. The cups and saucers are gathered
And stacked in the kitchen, the tray settled
With your tablets, a glass, a small jug of orange.
Are the windows shut, and all the doors locked?

I pass near the desk in my room and stand a minute
Looking down the notes I made this morning.
Yes: tomorrow it might do to begin.

The wall opposite is blank but alive
—Standing water over sunken currents.
The currents pursue their slow eddies through the house
Scarcely loosening as yet the objects of our love.

Soon the Falls will thunder, our love's detritus
Slide across the brim seriatim, glittering,
And vanish, swallowed into that insane
White roar. Chaos. All battered, scattered.

Yes: in the morning I will put on the cataract,
Give it veins, clutching hands, the short shriek of thought.

Magnanimity
(for Austin Clarke's seventieth birthday)

> 'So I forgot
> His enmity.'

Green abundance
Last summer in Coole Park. A stone hearth
Surviving; a grassy path by the orchard wall.

You stared through chicken-wire at the initials
Cut in Lady Gregory's tree, scars grown thick.
Overhead a breath passed magniloquently through the leaves,

Branches swayed and sank. You turned away and said
Coole might be built again as a place for poets.
Through the forbidden tree magnanimity passed.

I am sure that there are no places for poets,
Only changing habitations for verse to outlast.
Your own house, isolated by a stream, exists

For your use while you live—like your body and your world.
Helpless commonness encroaches, chews the soil,
Squats ignobly. Within, consciousness intensifies:

Sharp small evils magnify into Evil,
Pity and mockery suggest some idea of Good,
Fright stands up stiffly under pain of death.

Houses shall pass away, and all give place
To signposts and chicken-wire.
                                    A tree stands.
Pale cress persists on a shaded stream.

The Poet Egan O'Rahilly, Homesick in Old Age

He climbed to his feet in the cold light, and began
The decrepit progress again, blown along the cliff road,
Bent with curses above the shrew his stomach.

The salt abyss poured through him, more raw
With every laboured, stony crash of the waves:
His teeth bared at their voices, that incessant dying.

Iris leaves bent on the ditch, unbent,
Shivering in the wind: leaf-like spirits
Chattered at his death-mark as he passed.

He pressed red eyelids: aliens crawled
Breaking princely houses in their jaws;
Their metal faces reared up, eating at light.

'Princes overseas, who slipped away
In your extremity, no matter where I travel
I find your great houses like stopped hearts.

73

Likewise your starving children—though I nourish
Their spirit, and my own, on the lists of praises
I make for you still in the cooling den of my craft.

Our enemies multiply. They have recruited the sea:
Last night, the West's rhythmless waves destroyed my sleep;
This morning, winkle and dogfish persisting in the stomach . . .'

'To Autumn'

Insect beads crawl on the warm soil,
Black carapaces; brittle harvest spiders
Clamber weightlessly among dry roots
In soundless bedlam. He sits still writing
At the edge of the wheatfield, a phantasm of flesh

while thy hook
Spares . . .

Ripened leagues, a plain of odorous seed,
Quiet scope, season of mastery,
The last of peace. Along ethereal summits,
A gleam of disintegrating materials
Held a frail instant at unearthly heights.

Soft Toy

I am soiled with the repetition of your loves and hatreds
      And other experiments. You do not hate me,
Crumpled in my corner. You do not love me,
      A small heaped corpse. My face of beaten fur
Responds as you please: if you do not smile
      It does not smile; to impatience or distaste
It answers blankness, beyond your goodwill
      —Blank conviction, beyond your understanding or mine.

I lie limp with use and re-use, listening.
Loose ends of conversations, hesitations,
Half-beginnings that peter out in my presence,
Are enough. I understand, with a flame of shame
Or a click of ease or joy, inert. Knowledge
Into resignation: the process drives deeper,
Grows clearer, eradicating chance growths of desire.
And colder: all possibilities of desire.

My button-brown hard eyes fix on your need
To grow, as you crush me with tears and throw me aside.
Most they reflect, but something absorb—brightening
In response, with energy, to the energy of your changes.
Clutched tightly through the night, held before you,
Ragged and quietly crumpled, as you thrust, are thrust,
In dull terror into your opening brain,
I face the dark with eyes that cannot close
—The cold, outermost points of your will, as you sleep.
Between your tyrannous pressure and the black
Resistance of the void my blankness hardens
To a blunt probe, a cold pitted grey face.

Leaf-Eater

On a shrub in the heart of the garden,
On an outer leaf, a grub twists
Half its body, a tendril,
This way and that in blind
Space: no leaf or twig
Anywhere in reach; then gropes
Back on itself and begins
To eat its own leaf.

Nightwalker

Mindful of the shambles of the day
    But mindful under the blood's drowsy humming
Of will that gropes for structure; nonetheless
    Not unmindful of the madness without,
The madness within—the book of reason
    Slammed open, slammed shut:

1

I only know things seem and are not good.

A brain in the dark, and bones, out exercising
Shadowy flesh. Fitness for the soft belly,
Fresh air for lungs that take no pleasure any longer.
The smell of gardens under suburban lamplight,
Clipped privet, a wall blotted with shadows
—Monsters of ivy squat in lunar glare.

There above the roofs it hangs,
A mask of grey dismay. Like a fat skull,
Or the pearl knob of a pendulum
At the outermost reach of its swing, about to detach
Its hold on the upper night, for the return.
That dark area the mark of Cain.

*

My shadow twists about my feet in the light
Of every passing street lamp. Window after window
Pale entities, motionless in their cells like grubs,
Wait in a blue trance:

                                        Near Necropolis.
A laboratory underground. Embalmers,
Their arms toiling in unearthly light,
Their mouths opening and closing.
                                        A shade enters,
Patrolling the hive of his brain.

*

I must lie down with them all soon and sleep,
And rise with them again when the new day
Has roused us. We'll come scratching in our waistcoats
Down to the kitchen for a cup of tea.
Then with our briefcases, by the neighbours' gardens,
To wait at the station, assembled for the day's toil,
Fluttering our papers, palping the cool wind.
Ready to serve our businesses and government
As together we develop our community
On clear principles, with no fixed ideas.
And (twitching our thin umbrellas) agreeable
That during a transitional period
Development should express itself in forms
Without principle, based on fixed ideas.

Robed in spattered iron she stands
At the harbour mouth, Productive Investment,
And beckons the nations through our gold half-door:
Lend me your wealth, your cunning and your drive,
Your arrogant refuse. Let my people serve them
Holy water in our new hotels,
While native businessmen and managers
Drift with them chatting over to the window
To show them our growing city, give them a feeling
Of what is possible; our labour pool,
The tax concessions to foreign capital,
How to get a nice estate though German.
Even collect some of our better young artists.

*

Spirit shapes are climbing into view
At the end of the terrace. You can pick them out,
With their pale influences.

The Wakeful Twins.
Bruder und Schwester . . .
Two young Germans I had in this morning
Wanting to transfer investment income.
The sister a business figurehead, her brother
Otterfaced, with exasperated smiles
Assuming—pressing until he achieved—response.
Handclasp; I do not exist; I cannot take my eyes
From their pallor. A red glare plays on their faces,
Livid with little splashes of blazing fat.
The oven door closes.

All about and above me
The officials on the corridors or in their rooms
Work, or overwork, with mixed motives
Or none; dominate, entering middle age;
Subserve, aborting vague tendencies
With buttery smiles.
Among us, behind locked doors,
The ministers are working, with a sureness of touch
Found in the nation's birth—the blood of enemies
And brothers dried on their hide long ago.
Dragon old men, upright and stately and blind,
Or shuffling in the corridor finding a key,
What occupies them as they sit in their rooms?
What they already are? Shadow flesh.
Linked into constellations with their dead.

Look! The Wedding Group . . .
The Groom, the Best Man, the Fox, and their three ladies.
A tragic tale. Soon, the story tells,
Enmity sprang up between them, and the Fox
Took to the wilds. Then, to the Groom's sorrow,
His dear friend left him also, vowing hatred.

So they began destroying the Groom's substance
And he sent out to hunt the Fox, but trapped
His friend instead; mourning he slaughtered him.
Shortly, in his turn, the Groom was savaged
No one knows by whom. Though it's known the Fox
Is a friend of death, and rues nothing.

                         There, in the same quarter,
The Two Executioners—Groom and Weasel—
'77' burning onto each brow.
And there the Weasel again, dancing crookbacked
Under the Player King.

                   A tragicomical tale:
How the Fox discovered a golden instrument,
A great complex gold horn, left at his door.
He examined it with little curiosity,
Wanting no gold or music; observed the mouthpiece,
Impossible to play with fox's lips,
And gave it with dull humour to his old enemy,
The Weasel. Who bared his needle teeth,
Recognising the horn of the Player King.
He took it, hammered on it with a stick,
And pranced about in blithe pantomime,
His head cocked to enjoy the golden clouts.
While the Fox from time to time nodded his mask.

2

The human taste grows faint, leaving a taste
Of self and laurel leaves and salt. Gardens
Smelling of sand and half-stripped rocks in the dark.
Big snails glistening among roots of iris.

A cast-iron lamp standard sheds yellow light
On the sea wall. A page of today's paper
Lifts in the gutter.
                  Our new young minister
Glares in his hunting suit, white haunch on haunch.

Other lamps are lighting along a terrace
Of high Victorian houses, toward the tower
Rising into the dark at the Forty Foot.
The tide is drawing back from the promenade
Far as the lamplight can reach, into a dark
Alive with signals. Little bells in the channel
Beyond the rocks; Howth twinkling across the Bay;
Ships' lights moving along invisible sea lanes;
The Bailey light sweeping the middle distance,
Flickering on something.

*

               Watcher in the tower,
Be with me now. Turn your milky spectacles
On the sea, unblinking.

               A dripping cylinder
Pokes up into sight, picked out by the moon.
Two blazing eyes. Two tough shoulders of muscle
Lit from within by joints and bones of light.
Another head: animal, with nostrils
Straining open, red as embers. Goggle eyes.
A phantom whinny. Forehooves scrape at the night.
A spectral stink of horse and rider's sweat.
The rider grunts and urges.

               Father of Authors!
It is himself! In silk hat, accoutred
In stern jodhpurs. The Sonhusband
Coming in his power, climbing the dark
To his mansion in the sky, to take his place
In the influential circle, mounting to glory
On his big white harse!

A new sign: Foxhunter.
Subjects will find the going hard but rewarding.
You may give offence, but this should pass.
Marry the Boss's daughter.

*

The soiled paper settles back in the gutter.
THE NEW IRELAND . . .
                    Awkward in the saddle

But able and willing for the foul ditch,
And sitting as well as any at the kill,
Whatever iron Faust opens the gate.

It is begun: curs mill and yelp at your heel,
Backsnapping and grinning. They eye your back.
Beware the smile of the dog.

                    But you know the breed,
And all it takes to turn them
To a pack of lickspittles running as one.

3

The foot of the tower. An angle where the darkness
Is complete. A backdrop of constellations,
Crudely done and mainly unfamiliar.
They are arranged to suggest a chart of the brain.

In the part of the little harbour that can be seen
The moon is reflected in low water. Beyond,
A line of lamps on the terrace. Music far off.

Lung tips flutter. Out of the vest's darkness
The smell of my body: chalk dust and flowers.
Faint brutality.
                    The creak of shoes.
The loins of Brother Burke against our desk:

. . . And Dublin Castle used the National Schools
To try to conquer the Irish national spirit
At the same time exterminating our 'jargon'
—The Irish language, in which Saint Patrick, Saint Bridget
And Saint Colmcille taught and prayed!
Edmund Ignatius Rice founded our Order
To provide schools that were national in more than name.
Pupils from our schools have played their part
In the fight for freedom. And you will be called
In your various ways. To work for the native language.
To show your love by *working* for your country.
Today there are past pupils everywhere
In the Government service. Ministers of State
Have sat where some of you are sitting now.
It wasn't long before her Majesty
Gave us the Famine—the Starvation, as Bernard Shaw,
A godless writer, called it more correctly . . .

Bread of certainty. Soup of memories
In a dish of scalding tears. The food of dragons
And my own dragon half.
                        The Blessed Virgin
Smiles from her pedestal, like young Victoria.
Celibates, adolescents, we make our vows
To God and Ireland in her name, thankful
That by our studies here they may not lack
Civil servants in a state of grace.

A seamew passes over whingeing: *Eire,
Eire. Is there none to hear? Is all lost?*
Not yet all. A while still your voice . . .

*Alas, I think I will dash myself at the stones.
I will become a wind on the sea.
Or a wave of the sea again, or a sea sound.*

*At the first light of the sun I stirred on my rock.
I have seen the sun go down at the end of the world.
Now I fly across the face of the moon.*

Sad music fills the scene. A dying language
Echoes across a century's silence.
It is time I turned for home.

Her dear shadow on the blind. The breadknife.
She was slicing and buttering a loaf of bread.
My heart stopped. I starved for speech.

I believe now that love is half persistence,
A medium in which from change to change
Understanding may be gathered.

Hesitant, cogitating, exit.

4

Moon of my dismay, Virgin most pure,
Reflected enormous in her shaggy pool,
Quiet as oil. My brain swims in her light
And gathers into a book beneath her stare.
She reads and her mask darkens.
But she soon brightens a little:

It was a terrible time.
Nothing but horrors of one kind and another.
My tears flowed again and again.
But we came to take the waters, and when I drank
I felt my patience and trust coming back.

From time to time it seems that everything
Is breaking down. But we must never despair.
There are times it is all part of a meaningful drama
Beginning in the grey mists of antiquity
And reaching through the years to unknown goals
In the consciousness of man, which makes it less gloomy.

A wind sighs. The pool shivers. The tide
At the turn. Odour of lamplight, and the sea bed,
Passing like a ghost. She rules on high,
Queenlike, pale with control.

Hatcher of peoples!
Incline from your darkness into mine.
I stand at the ocean's edge, my head fallen back
Heavy with your control, and oppressed.

5

A pulse hisses in my ear.
                              I am an arrow
Piercing the void, unevenly as I correct

And correct. But swift as thought.
I arrive enveloped in quiet.
I believe I have heard of this place.

A true desert, sterile and odourless.
Naked to every peril. A bluish light
Beats down, to kill every bodily thing.

But the shadows are alive. They scuttle and flicker
Across the surface searching for sick spirits,
Sucking at their dry juices.

I think this is the Sea of Disappointment.
If I stoop down, and touch the edge, it has
A human taste, of massed human wills.

Ritual of Departure

1

Open the soft string that clasps in series
A dozen silver spoons, and spread them out,
Matched perfectly, one maker and to the year,
Brilliant in use from the first inheritor.

A stag crest stares from the soft solid silver
With fat cud lips and jaws that could crack bones.
The stag heart stumbles, rearing at bay,
Rattling a trophied head, slavering silver.

*

A portico, beggars moving on the steps.
A horserider locked in soundless greeting,
Bowed among dogs and dung. A panelled vista
Closing on pleasant smoke-blue far-off hills.

The same city distinct in the same air,
More open in an earlier evening light,
In sweet-breathing death-ease after forced Union.
Domes, pillared, in the afterglow.

2

The ground opens. Pale wet potatoes
Fall into light. The black soil falls from their flesh,
From the hands that tear them up and spread them out,
Perishable roots to eat.

Fields dying away
Among white rock and red bog—saturated
High places traversed by spring sleet,
Thrust up through the thin wind into pounding silence.

Farther South: landscape with ancestral figures.
Names settling and intermixing on the earth.
The seed in slow retreat into bestial silence.
Faces sharpen and grow blank, with eyes for nothing.

*

And their children's children vanished in the city lanes.

I saw the light enter from the laneway
Through the scullery, and creep to the foot of the stairs
Over grey floorboards, and sink in plush
In the staleness of an inner room.

I scoop at the earth and sense famine,
A sourness in the clay. The roots tear softly.

3

A man at the moment of departure, turning
To leave, treasures some stick of furniture
With slowly blazing eyes, or the very door
Broodingly with his hand as it falls shut.

Phoenix Park

The Phaenix builds the Phaenix' nest.
  Love's architecture is his own.

1

One stays or leaves. The one who returns is not
The one, etcetera. And we are leaving.
You are quiet and watchful, this last visit.
We pass the shapes of cattle blurred by moisture;
A few deer lift up their wet horns from the grass;

A smoke-soft odour of graves . . . our native damp.
A twig with two damp leaves drops on the bonnet
From the upper world, trembling; shows us its clean
Fracture and vanishes, snatched off by the wind:
Droplets of moisture shudder on the windscreen.

—You start at the suddenness, as though it were
Your own delicate distinct flesh that had snapped.
What was in your thoughts . . . saying, after a while,
I write you nothing, no love songs, any more?
Fragility echoing fragilities . . .

The Chapelizod Gate. Dense trees on our right,
Sycamores and chestnuts around the entrance
To St Mary's Hospital. Under their shade
I entered long ago, took the twisting paths
To find you by the way of hesitation.

You lay still, brilliant with illness, behind glass;
I stooped and tasted your life until you woke,
And your body's fever leaped out at my mind.
There's a fever now that eats everything
—Everything but the one positive dream.

That dream: it is something I might offer you.
Sorry it is not anything for singing;
Your body would know that it is positive
—Everything you know you know bodily.
And the preparation also. Take them both.

The preparation

Near a rounded wooded hillock, where a stream
Drains under the road, inside Islandbridge Gate,
A child stooped to the grass, picking and peeling
And devouring mushrooms straight out of the ground:
Death-pallor in their dry flesh, the taste of death.

Later, in freezing darkness, I came alone
To the railings round the Pond; whispered *Take me,
I am nothing*. But the words hovered, their sense
Revealing opposite within opposite.
Understanding moved, a silent bright discus.

As, when I walked this glimmering road, it did
Once, between night-trees. The stars seemed in my grasp,
Changing places among the naked branches
—Thoughts drawing into order under night's skull.
But something moved on the path: faint, sweet breathing—

A woman stood, thin and tired, in a light dress,
And interrupted kindly, in vague hunger.
Her hand rested for a moment on my sleeve.
I studied her and saw shame does not matter,
Nor kindness when there's no answering hunger

And passed by; her eyes burned . . . So equipped to learn
I found you, in feverish sleep, where you lay.
Midsummer, and I had tasted your knowledge,
My flesh blazing in yours; Autumn, I had learned
Giving without tearing is not possible.

*

The Furry Glen: grass sloping down to the lake,
Where she stooped in her Communion finery,
Our first-born, Sara in innocence, and plucked
Something out of the ground for us to admire.
The child smiled in her white veil, self-regarding.

2

We leave the Park through the Knockmaroon Gate and turn,
Remembering, downhill to the Liffey road
With the ache of dampness growing in our lungs.
Along river curves sunk under heavy scenes,
By the Strawberry Beds, under gravel slopes,

To sit drinking in a back bar in Lucan
At a glass table, under a staring light,
Talking of departure. You are uneasy;
I make signs on the surface with my wet glass
In human regret, but human certainty:

Whatever the ultimate grotesqueries
They'll have to root in more than this sour present.
The ordeal-cup, set at each turn, so far
We have welcomed, sour or sweet. What matter where
It waits for us next, if we will take and drink?

The dream

Look into the cup: the tissues of order
Form under your stare. The living surfaces
Mirror each other, gather everything
Into their crystalline world. Figure echoes
Figure faintly in the saturated depths;

Revealed by faint flashes of each other
They light the whole confines: a fitful garden . . .
A child plucks death and tastes it; a shade watches
Over him, the child fades and the shade, made flesh,
Stumbles on understanding, begins to fade,

Bequeathing a child in turn; women-shapes pass
Unseeing, full of knowledge, through each other
. . . All gathered. And the crystal so increases,
Eliciting in its substance from the dark
The slowly forming laws it increases by.

89

Laws of order I find I have discovered
Mainly at your hands. Of failure and increase.
The stagger and recovery of spirit:
That life is hunger, hunger is for order,
And hunger satisfied brings on new hunger

Till there's nothing to come;—let the crystal crack
On some insoluble matter, then its heart
Shudders and accepts the flaw, adjusts on it
Taking new strength—given the positive dream;
Given, with your permission, undying love.

That, while the dream lasts, there's a total hunger
That gropes out disappearing just past touch,
A blind human face burrowing in the void,
Eating new tissue down into existence
Until every phantasm—all that can come—

Has roamed in flesh and vanished, or passed inward
Among the echoing figures to its place,
And this live world is emptied of its hunger
While the crystal world, undying, crowds with light,
Filling the cup . . . That there is one last phantasm

Who'll come painfully in old lewd nakedness
—Loose needles of bone coming out through his fat—
Groping with an opposite, equal hunger,
Thrusting a blind skull from its tatters of skin
As from a cowl, to smile in understanding

And total longing; aching to plant one kiss
In the live crystal as it aches with fullness,
And accommodate his body with that kiss;
But that forever he will pause, the final
Kiss ungiveable. Giving without tearing

Is not possible; to give totality
Is to be torn totally, a nothingness
Reaching out in stasis a pure nothingness.
—Therefore everlasting life, the unmoving
Stare of full desire. Given undying love.

*

I give them back not as your body knows them
—That flesh is finite, so in love we persist;
That love is to clasp simply, question fiercely;
That getting life we eat pain in each other.
But mental, in my fever—mere idea.

3

Our glasses drained, we finish and rise to go,
And stand again in the saturated air
Near the centre of the village, breathing in
Faint smells of chocolate and beer, fallen leaves
In the gutter, bland autumnal essences.

You wait a minute on the path, absently
—Against massed brown trees—tying a flimsy scarf
At your neck. Fair Ellinor. O Christ thee save.
And I taste a structure, ramshackle, ghostly,
Vanishing on my tongue, given and taken,

Distinct. A ghost of that ghost persists, structure
Without substance, all about us, in the air,
Among the trees, before us at the crossroads,
On the stone bridge, insinuating itself
Into being. Undying . . . And I shiver

Seeing your thoughtless delicate completeness.
Love, it is certain, continues till we fail,
Whenever (with your forgiveness) that may be
—At any time, now, totally, ordeal
Succeeding ordeal till we find some death,

Hoarding bitterness, or refusing the cup;
Then the vivifying eye clouds, and the thin
Mathematic tissues loosen, and the cup
Thickens, and order dulls and dies in love's death
And melts away in a hungerless no dream.

*

Fragility echoing fragilities
From whom I have had every distinctness
Accommodate me still, where—folded in peace
And undergoing with ghostly gaiety
Inner immolation, shallowly breathing—

You approach the centre by its own sweet light.
I consign my designing will stonily
To your flames. Wrapped in that rosy fleece, two lives
Burn down around one love, one flickering-eyed
Stone self becomes more patient than its own stone.

*

The road divides and we can take either way,
Etcetera. The Phoenix Park; Inchicore,
Passing Phoenix Street—the ways are one, sweet choise,
Our selves become our own best sacrifice.
Continue, so. We'll perish in each other.

4

The tyres are singing, cornering back and forth
In our green world again; into groves of trees,
By lake and open park, past the hospital.
The west ignites behind us; round one more turn
Pale light in the east hangs over the city:

An eighteenth-century prospect to the sea—
River haze; gulls; spires glitter in the distance
Above faint multitudes. Barely audible
A murmur of soft, wicked laughter rises.
Dublin, the umpteenth city of confusion.

A theatre for the quick articulate,
The agonized genteel, their artful watchers.
Malice as entertainment. Asinine feast
Of sowthistles and brambles! And there dead men,
Half hindered by dead men, tear down dead beauty.

Return by the mental ways we have ourselves
Established, past visages of memory
Set at every turn: where we smiled and passed
Without a second thought, or stood in the rain
And whispered bitterly; where we roamed at night

Drunk in joyful love, looking for enemies
(They in our bodies—white handkerchief, white page,
Crimsoned with panic); where naked by firelight
We stood and rested from each other and took
Our burden from the future, eyes crystalline,

My past alive in you, a gift of tissue
Torn free from my life in an odour of books.
That room . . . The shapes of tiredness had assembled
Long ago in its four dark corners, before
You came, waiting, while you were everywhere.

One midnight at the starlit sill I let them
Draw near. Loneliness drew into order:
A thought of fires in the hearts of darknesses,
A darkness at the heart of every fire,
Darkness, fire, darkness, threaded on each other—

The orders of stars fixed in abstract darkness,
Darknesses of worlds sheltering in their light;
World darkness harbouring orders of cities,
Whose light at midnight harbours human darkness;
The human dark pierced by solitary fires . . .

Such fires as one I have seen gutter and fail
And, as it sank, reveal the fault in its heart
Opening on abstract darkness, where hunger
Came with gaping kiss over terrible wastes
—Till the flames sprang up and blindness was restored.

Attracted from the night by my wakefulness
Certain half-dissolved—half-formed—beings loomed close:
A child with eaten features eating something—
Another, with unfinished features, in white—
They hold hands. A shadow bends to protect them.

The shadow tries to speak, but its tongue stumbles.
A snake out of the void moves in my mouth, sucks
At triple darkness. A few ancient faces
Detach and begin to circle. Deeper still,
Delicate distinct tissue begins to form,

NEW POEMS (1973)

hesitate, cease to exist, glitter again,
dither in and out of a mother liquid
on the turn, welling up from God knows what hole.

Dear God, if I had known how far and deep,
how long and cruel, I think my being
would have blanched: appalled.
                                        How artless,
how loveless I was then! O dear, dear God,
the times I had in my disarray—cooped up
with the junk of centuries! The excitement,
underlining and underlining in that narrow room!
—dust (all that remained of something) settling
in the air over my pleasures.
                                        Many a time
I have risen from my gnawed books
and prowled about, wrapped in a long grey robe,
and rubbed my forehead; reached for my instruments
—canister and kettle, the long-handled spoon,
metal vessels and delph; settled the flame,
blue and yellow; and, in abstracted hunger,
my book propped before me, eaten forkfuls
of scrambled egg and buttered fresh bread
and taken hot tea until the sweat stood out
at the roots of my hair!
                                        Then, getting quietly ready
to go down quietly out of my mind,
I have lain down on the soiled divan
alert as though for a journey

and turned to things not right nor reasonable.
At such a time I wouldn't thank
the Devil himself to knock at my door.

*

The key, though I hardly knew it,
        already in my fist.
Falling. Mind darkening.
        Toward a ring of mouths.

Flushed.
            Time, distance,
        Meaning nothing.
                    No matter.

*

I don't know how long I may have fallen
in terror of the uprushing floor
in my shell of solitude
when I became aware of certain rods of iron
laid down side by side, as if by giants,
in what had seemed the solid rock.
With what joy did I not hope, suddenly,
I might pass through unshattered
—to whatever Pit! But I fell foul at the last
and broke in a distress of gilt and silver,
scattered in a million droplets of
fright and loneliness . . .
                    So sunless.
That sour coolness . . . So far from the world and earth . . .
No bliss, no pain; dullness after pain.
A cistern-hiss . . . A thick tunnel stench
rose to meet me. Frightful. Dark nutrient waves.
And I knew no more.

96

When I came to,
the air I drifted in trembled around me
to a vast distance with sighs
—not from any great grief, but disturbed
by countless forms drifting as I did,
wavery albumen bodies
each burdened with an eye. Poor spirits!
How tentative and slack our search
along the dun shore whose perpetual hiss
breaks softly, and breaks again,
on endless broken shells! Stare as we will
with our red protein eyes, how few we discover
that are whole—a shell here and there
among so many—to slip into and grow blank!
Once more all faded.
                              I was alone,
nearing the heart of the pit,
the light growing fitfully more bright.
A pale fume beat steadily through the gloom.
I saw, presently, it was a cauldron:
ceaselessly over its lip a vapour of forms
curdled, glittered and vanished. Soon I made out
a ring of mountainous beings staring upward
with open mouths—naked ancient women.
Nothingness silted under their thighs
and over their limp talons. I confess
my heart, as I stole through to my enterprise,
hammered in fear.
                              And then I raised my eyes
to that seemingly unattainable grill
through which I must return, carrying my prize.

Hen Woman

The noon heat in the yard
smelled of stillness and coming thunder.
A hen scratched and picked at the shore.
It stopped, its body crouched and puffed out.
The brooding silence seemed to say 'Hush . . .'

The cottage door opened,
a black hole
in a whitewashed wall so bright
the eyes narrowed.
Inside, a clock murmured 'Gong . . .'

(I had felt all this before.)

She hurried out in her slippers
muttering, her face dark with anger,
and gathered the hen up jerking
languidly. Her hand fumbled.
Too late. Too late.

It fixed me with its pebble eyes
(seeing what mad blur).
A white egg showed in the sphincter;
mouth and beak opened together;
and time stood still.

Nothing moved: bird or woman,
fumbled or fumbling—locked there
(as I must have been) gaping.

*

There was a tiny movement at my feet,
tiny and mechanical; I looked down.
A beetle like a bronze leaf
was inching across the cement,
clasping with small tarsi
a ball of dung bigger than its body.

The serrated brow pressed the ground humbly,
lifted in a short stare, bowed again;
the dung-ball advanced minutely,
losing a few fragments,
specks of staleness and freshness.

*

A mutter of thunder far off
—time not quite stopped.
I saw the egg had moved a fraction:
a tender blank brain
under torsion, a clean new world.

As I watched, the mystery completed.
The black zero of the orifice
closed to a point
and the white zero of the egg hung free,
flecked with greenish brown oils.

It fell and turned over slowly.
Dreamlike, fussed by her splayed fingers,
it floated outward, moon-white,
leaving no trace in the air,
and began its drop to the shore.

*

I feed upon it still, as you see;
there is no end to that which, not understood,
may yet be hoarded in the imagination,
in the yolk of one's being, so to speak,
there to undergo its (quite animal) growth,

dividing blindly, twitching, packed with will,
searching in its own tissue
for the structure in which it may wake.
Something that had—clenched in its cave—
not been now was: an egg of being.

Through what seemed a whole year it fell
—as it still falls, for me, solid and light,
the red gold beating in its silvery womb,
alive as the yolk and white of my eye.
As it will continue to fall, probably, until I die,
through the vast indifferent spaces
with which I am empty.

*

It smashed against the grating
and slipped down quickly out of sight.
It was over in a comical flash.
The soft mucous shell clung a little longer,
then drained down.

She stood staring, in blank anger.
Then her eyes came to life, and she laughed
and let the bird flap away.

It's all the one.
There's plenty more where that came from!

A Hand of Solo

Lips and tongue
wrestle the delicious
    life out of you.

A last drop.
Wonderful.
    A moment's rest.

In the firelight glow
the flickering
    shadows softly

come and go up on the shelf:
red heart and black spade
    hid in the kitchen dark.

Woman throat song
help my head
        back to you sweet.

*

Hushed, buried green baize.
Slide and stop. Black spades. Tray. Still.
Red deuce. Two hearts. Blood-clean. Still.

Black flash. Jack Rat grins.
She drops down. Silent. Face disk blank. Queen.

The Boss spat in the kitchen fire.
His head shook.

Angus's fat hand brushed in all the pennies.
His waistcoat pressed the table.

Uncle Matty slithered the cards together
and knocked them. Their edges melted. Soft gold.

Angus picked up a bright penny and put it
in my hand: satiny, dream-new disk of light . . .

'Go on out in the shop and get yourself something.'
'Now, Angus . . .'
                'Now, now, Jack. He's my luck.'
'Tell your grandmother we're waiting for her.'

She was settling the lamp.
Two yellow tongues rose and brightened.
The shop brightened.

Her eyes glittered.
A tin ghost beamed, Mick McQuaid
nailed across the fireplace.

'Shut the kitchen door, child of grace.
Come here to me.
Come here to your old grandmother.'

Strings of jet beads wreathed her neck
and hissed on the black taffeta
and crept on my hair.

'. . . You'd think I had three heads!'
My eyes were squeezed shut against the key
in the pocket of her apron. Her stale abyss . . .

Old knuckles pressed on the counter,
then were snatched away. She sat down at the till
on her high stool, chewing nothing.

The box of Indian apples
was over in the corner
by the can of oil.

I picked out one of the fruit,
a rose-red hard wax
turning toward gold, light like wood,

and went at it with little bites,
peeling off bits of skin
and tasting the first traces of the blood.

When it was half peeled,
with the glassy pulp exposed like cells,
I sank my teeth in it

loosening the packed mass of dryish beads
from their indigo darkness.
I drove my tongue among them

and took a mouthful, and slowly
bolted them. My throat filled
with a rank, Arab bloodstain.

Ancestor

I was going up to say something,
and stopped. Her profile against the curtains
was old, and dark like a hunting bird's.

It was the way she perched on the high stool,
staring into herself, with one fist
gripping the side of the barrier around her desk
—or her head held by something, from inside.
And not caring for anything around her
or anyone there by the shelves.
I caught a faint smell, musky and queer.

I may have made some sound—she stopped rocking
and pressed her fist in her lap; then she stood up
and shut down the lid of the desk, and turned the key.
She shoved a small bottle under her aprons
and came toward me, darkening the passageway.

Ancestor . . . among sweet- and fruit-boxes.
Her black heart . . .
                          Was that a sigh?
—brushing by me in the shadows,
with her heaped aprons, through the red hangings
to the scullery, and down to the back room.

Tear

I was sent in to see her.
A fringe of jet drops
chattered at my ear
as I went in through the hangings.

I was swallowed in chambery dusk.
My heart shrank
at the smell of disused
organs and sour kidney.

The black aprons I used to
bury my face in
were folded at the foot of the bed
in the last watery light from the window

(Go in and say goodbye to her)
and I was carried off
to unfathomable depths.
I turned to look at her.

She stared at the ceiling
and puffed her cheek, distracted,
propped high in the bed
resting for the next attack.

The covers were gathered close
up to her mouth,
that the lines of ill-temper still
marked. Her grey hair

was loosened out like a young woman's
all over the pillow,
mixed with the shadows
criss-crossing her forehead

and at her mouth and eyes,
like a web of strands tying down her head
and tangling down toward the shadow
eating away the floor at my feet.

I couldn't stir at first, nor wished to,
for fear she might turn and tempt me
(my own father's mother)
with open mouth

—with some fierce wheedling whisper—
to hide myself one last time
against her, and bury my
self in her drying mud.

Was I to kiss her? As soon
kiss the damp that crept
in the flowered walls
of this pit.

Yet I had to kiss.
I knelt by the bulk of the death bed
and sank my face in the chill
and smell of her black aprons.

Snuff and musk, the folds against my eyelids,
carried me into a derelict place
smelling of ash: unseen walls and roofs
rustled like breathing.

I found myself disturbing
dead ashes for any trace
of warmth, when far off
in the vaults a single drop

splashed. And I found
what I was looking for
—not heat nor fire,
not any comfort,

but her voice, soft, talking to someone
about my father: 'God help him, he cried
big tears over there by the machine
for the poor little thing.' Bright

drops on the wooden lid
for my infant sister.
My own wail of child-animal grief
was soon done, with any early guess

at sad dullness and tedious pain
and lives bitter with hard bondage.
How I tasted it now—
her heart beating in my mouth!

She drew an uncertain breath
and pushed at the clothes
and shuddered tiredly.
I broke free

and left the room
promising myself
when she was really dead
I would really kiss.

My grandfather half looked up
from the fireplace as I came out,
and shrugged and turned back
with a deaf stare to the heat.

I fidgeted beside him for a minute
and went out to the shop.
It was still bright there
and I felt better able to breathe.

Old age can digest
anything: the commotion
at Heaven's gate—the struggle
in store for you all your life.

How long and hard it is
before you get to Heaven,
unless like little Agnes
you vanish with early tears.

The High Road

Don't be too long now, the next time.
She hugged me tight in behind the counter.
Here! she whispered.
                                        A silvery
little mandoline, out of the sweet-box.

They were standing waiting in the sun outside
at the shop door, with the go car,
their long shadows along the path.

A horse trotted past us down Bow Lane:
Padno Carty sat in the trap
sideways, fat, drifting along
with a varnish twinkle of spokes
and redgold balls of manure scattering
behind on the road.

Mrs Fullerton was sitting on a stool
in her doorway, beak-nosed, one eye dead.
DAAARK! squawked the sour parrot in her room.
Sticking to his cage with slow nails, upside down;
creeping stiffly crossways, with his tongue
mumbling on a bar, a black moveable nut.

Silver tiny strings
trembled in my brain.

Over the parapet of the bridge
at the end of Granny and Granda's
the brown water bubbled and poured
over the stones and tin cans in the Camac,
down by the back of Aunty Josie's.

A stony darkness, after the bridge,
trickled down Cromwell's Quarters step by step,
along the foot of the wall from James's Street.
Through a barred window on one of the steps
a mob of shadows huddled in the Malt Stores
among the brick pillars and the dunes of grain,
watching the pitch drain out of their wounds.

I held hands up the High Road
inside on the path, beside the feathery grass,
and looked down through the paling, pulled downward
by a queer feeling. Down there . . . windows
below the road. Small front gardens
getting lower and lower.
                              Over on the other side.
a path slants up across the clay slope
and disappears into the Robbers' Den.
I crept up once to the big hole, full of fright,
and knelt on the clay to look inside.
It was only a hollow someone made,
with a dusty piece of man's dung, and bluebottles.

Not even in my mind
has one silvery string
picked a single sound.
And it will never.

Above the far-off back yards
the breeze gave a sigh: a sin happening.
I let go and stopped, and looked down
and let it fall into empty air
and watched it turning over with little flashes
silveryshivering with loss.

The Liffey Hill

The path climbs up to the left, toward the Plantation
—high tree trunks, a clay floor dim and still,
with papers and bottles caught in the roots.
Then to the right across the grass slope.
It opens at the top in a long field
narrowing down in bushes and wire at the far end

where the snow hushed
on Christmas morning
and we followed the tracks of rabbits
dotted along light and powdery
breathless with carefulness
the snow powdery pure
on the wool glove, detailed and soft.

The day lengthened, and the wool darkened
and smelled of cold.
                                    We are out too late.
Voices, far away, die in the air.

But there is still the pleasure
of going home, and the day closing in.
I climbed up on the wall in the lamplight
and hugged the wooden pillar, and slipped down.

My boots scuffled on the path,
echoing alone,
                            down the Lane.

Good Night

It is so peaceful at last:
the heat creeping through the house,
the floorboards reacting in the corner.

The voices in the next room
boom on in their cabinet.
Would you agree then we won't find any truths . . .

How it brings out every falseness.
There is one of them
laughing at a remark of his own.

—that we need as we don't need truth . . .

Relax, and the sounds of the house are all
flowing into one another, soothing and pleasant,
down this suddenly live brinegullet,
attached into nothing by every sense

the ear pounding
peering eye-apples unseeing
tongue and fingers outstretched
a soft animal light off the walls and floor
human thighs growing out of the smooth rock
and moving over each other down near their roots.

If you look closely
you can see the tender undermost muscle
forming out of the rock
the veins continuing inward
just visible under the skin
and (faintly lit from within)
clusters of soft arms gathering down
tiny open eyes, fingertips,
pursed mouths from the gloom,
minute drifting corruscations of hair,
glistening little gnat-crescents of light!

What essences disturbed from what
profounder nothingness, where monsters lift
soft self-conscious voices, urgent yet mannerly:

Please, I would remind . . .
Oblivion, our natural condition . . .

and feed us and feed in us
and coil and uncoil in our substance
so that in that they are there
we cannot know them, and that,
daylit, we are the monsters of our night,
and somewhere the monsters of our night
are here, in nightnothing
that our daylight feeds in and feeds,
wandering out of their cavern,
a low cry echoing—Camacamacamac . . .

Irwin Street

Morning sunlight—a patch of clear memory—
warmed the path and the crumbling brick wall
and stirred the weeds sprouting in the mortar.

A sparrow cowered on a doorstep.
Under the broken door the paw of a cat
reached out.

       White nails fastened in the feathers.
Aware—a distinct dream—as though
slowly making it happen.

With my schoolbooks in my hand,
I turned the corner into the avenue
between the high wire fence and the trees in the Hospital.

Under the leaves the road was empty and fragrant
with little lances of light.
He was coming toward me, my maker,

in a white jacket, and with my face.
How could he be there, at this hour?
Our steps hesitated in awkward greeting.

*

Wakening again upstairs.
I sat up on the edge of the bed,
my feet on the bare boards,
my hand in my pyjama trousers.

Touching the River

That nude kneeling so sad-seeming
on her shelf of moss
how timelessly—all sepia—

her arm reaches down
to let her fingers, affectedly trailing,
stick in the stopped brown water.

Rivery movement, clay-fresh;
light murmuring over the surface.
Our unstopped flesh and senses—how they vanish.

Though we kneel on the brink and drive our stare
down, now, into the current.
Though everywhere in the wet fields

the reeds are shivering
(one clump of them, I know,
nestling a lark's eggs in a hoof-print).

Nuchal
(a fragment)

'. . . down among the roots
like a half buried vase brimming over
with pure water, a film of clear brilliancy
spilling down its sides, rippling with reflections
of the four corners of the garden.
Fish-spirits slip down into the grass.
The grass welcomes them with a hiss
of movement and voices—its own snake-spirits.

On the last of the grass,
dreaming on one outstretched arm,
the woman lies smiling in her sleep.
Her arm dips over the brink
with the fingers trailing ladylike in the water.
The rivulet simply wanders up to her,
making to go past out of the garden,
and meets her fingers. Four sunlit ripples
lengthen out from them: and the stream
divides and subdivides into four,
moistening the first downward curve of the hill.

She has dreamed so long already . . .
Four great rivers creep across the plain
toward the four corners of that vast domain.

Eastward, a quiet river feeds the soil
till the soft banks crumble, caked with oil.
A sudden shine, out of eternal spring:
a crop of gold, with many a precious thing
—bdellium, seeking the pearl in its own breast,
the flower-figured onyx, the amethyst.

Southward (it seems of melted gold) a stream
flows toward the summer in a fiery gleam.

A third runs Westward in its deeper bed,
tigrish, through narrow gorges, winy red,
as though some heart toward which it ran (a vein)
drew it onward through that cruel terrain.

Lastly, a milkwhite river faring forth
in a slow flood, laughing, toward the North.

Four rivers reaching toward th'encircling sea,
that bitter basin
                where every . . .'

Survivor

High near the heart of the mountain there is a cavern.
There, under pressure in the darkness,
as the walls protest and give dryly,
sometimes you can hear minute dust-falls.
But there is no danger.
The cavern is a perfect shell of force;
the stresses that brought this place forth
maintain it.
It is spoken of, always,
in terms of mystery—our first home . . .
that there is a power holding this part of the mountain
subtly separate from the world, in firm hands;
that this cave escaped the Deluge;
that it will play some part on the Last Day.

Far back, a lost echoing
single drop:
the musk of glands
and bloody gates and alleys.

Claws sprang open
starred with pain.

*

Curled in self hate. Delicious.
Head heavy. Arm too heavy.
What is it, to suffer:
the dismal rock nourishes.
Draughts creep: shelter in them.
Deep misery: it is a pleasure.
Soil the self, lie still.

Something crept in once. A flame of cold
that crept under the back and under the head
huddled close in to the knees and belly.
Was that a dream?

*

A new beginning. An entire new world
floating on the ocean like a cloud,
distilled from sunlight and the crests of foam.

We were all thieves. In search of a land without sin,
that might go unpunished. And so prowling
the Northern portion of the known world,
toward the West (thinking
places answering each other on Earth
might answer in nature).

Late afternoon we came in sight
of promontories beautiful beyond description
and saw the sea gather in savage currents
and dash itself against the cliffs.

By twilight everything was destroyed,
the only survivors a shoal of women
spilled onto the shingle, and one man
that soon—as they lifted themselves up
and looked about them in the dusk—
they silently surrounded.

Paradise. No serpents. No noxious beasts.
No lions. No toads. No injurious rats
or dragons or scorpions. Only the she-wolf.

Perpetual twilight. A last outpost in the gloom.
A land of the dead. Sometimes
an otherworldly music sounded on the wind.

Everyone falling sick, after a time.
Thin voices, thin threads of some kind of sweetness
dissolving one by one in the blood.

Above the landing place the grass shivered
in the thin shale at the top of the path,
never again disturbed. Where the sun went down
there was a great rock in the sea.
The Hag. Squatting on the water,
her muzzle staring up at nothing.

*

I must remember
and be able some time to explain.

There is nothing here for sustenance.

Hair. Claws. Grey.
Naked. Wretch. Wither.

Endymion

At first there was nothing. Then a closed space.
Such light as there was showed him sleeping.
I stole nearer and bent down; the light grew brighter,
and I saw it came from the interplay of our two beings.
It blazed in silence as I kissed his eyelids.
I straightened up and it faded, from his pallor
and the ruddy walls with their fleshy thickenings
—great raw wings, curled—a huge owlet stare—
as a single drop echoed in the depths.

At the Crossroads

A dog's
body zipped
open and
stiff in
the grass.

They used to leave hanged men here.

A night when the moon is full
and swims with evil through the trees,
if you walk from the silent stone bridge
to the first crossroads and stand there,
do you feel that sad disturbance under the branches?
Three times I have been halted there
and had to whisper 'O Christ protect'
and not known whether my care was for myself
or some other hungry spirit.
Once by a great whiplash without sound.
Once by an unfelt shock at my ribs
as a phantom dagger stuck shuddering in nothing.
Once by a torch flare crackling
suddenly unseen in my face.
Three times, always at that same corner.
Never altogether the same. But the same.

Once when I had worked like a dull ox
in patience to the point of foolishness
I found myself rooted here, my thoughts
scattered by the lash Clarity:
the end of labour is in sacrifice,
the beast of burden in his shuddering prime
—or in leaner times any willing dogsbody.

A white face
stared from the
void, tilted over,
her mouth ready.

And all mouths everywhere so
in their need, turning on each furious
other. Flux of forms
in a great stomach: living meat torn off,
enduring in one mess of terror
every pang it sent through every thing
it ever, in shudders of pleasure, tore.

A white ghost flickered into being
and disappeared near the tree tops.
An owl in silent scrutiny
with blackness in her heart. She
who succeeds from afar . . .

                          The choice—
the drop with deadened wing-beats; some creature
torn and swallowed; her brain, afterward,
staring among the rafters in the dark
until hunger returns.

Sacrifice

Crowded steps, a sea of white faces
streaked with toil. The scrutiny is over,
in sunlight, terrible black and white.
There is the mark . . . In those streaks.
Their hands are on her.
Her friends gather.

The multitudes sigh and bless
and persuade her forward to her tears
in doomed excitement down the cup of light
onto her back on the washed bricks
with breasts held apart
and midriff fluttering in the sun.

The souls gather unseen, hovering
above the table, not interfering,
as it is done in a shivering flash.
The vivid pale solid of the breast
dissolves in a crimson flood.
The heart flops in its sty.

*

Never mind the hurt. I've never felt
so terribly alive, so ready, so gripped by love
—gloved fingers slippery next the heart!
Is it very difficult?
The blinding pain—when love goes direct

118

and wrenches at the heart-strings!
But the pangs quickly pass their maximum,
and then such a fount of tenderness!
Are you stuck? Let me arch back.

I love how you keep muttering 'You know now . . .'
—and your concern.
But you must finish it.
I lose my mind gladly, thinking:
the heart—in another's clutches!

We are each other's knowledge.
It is peace that counts, and knowledge brings peace,
even thrust crackling into the skull
and bursting with tongues of fire.
Peace. Love dying down, as love ascends.

I love your tender triumph, straightening up,
lifting your reddened sleeves.
The stain spreads downward through your great flushed pinions.
You are a real angel.
My heart is in your hands: mind it well.

*All is emptiness
and I must spin*

A vacancy in which, apparently,
I hang
        with severed senses

*

I have been in places . . . The floors crept,
an electric terror waited everywhere.
We were made to separate and strip.
My urine flowed in mild excitement.
Our hands touched in farewell.

How bring oneself to judge, or think,
so hurled onward! inward!

After a while there was a slight
but perceptible movement of the air.
It was not Death, but night.
Mountain coolness; a freshness of dew
on the face—tears of self forming.

*

I was lying in a vaulted place.
The cold air crept over long-abandoned floors,
carrying a taint of remote iron and dead ash.
Echo of voices. A distant door closed.

The sterile:
it is a whole matter in itself.

The Clearing

'. . . there is so little I can do any more
but it is nearly done . . .'

It is night. A troubled figure
is moving about its business
muttering between the fire and the gloom.
Impenetrable growth surrounds him.
Owlful. Batful.
Great moths of prey.

'. . . and still the brainworm will not sleep
squirming behind the eyes
staring out from its narrow box . . .'

He stops suddenly and straightens.
The eyes grow sharper
—and the teeth!

'. . . and then the great ease
when something that was stalking us
is taken—the head cut off
held by the fur
the blood dropping hot
the eye-muscles star-bright to my jaws!'

Death Bed

Motionless—his sons—
we watched his brows draw together with strain.
The wind tore at the leather walls of our tent;
two grease lamps fluttered
at the head and foot of the bed.
Our shadows sprang here and there.

At that moment our sign might
have coursed across the heavens,
and we had spared no one to watch.

*

Our people are most vulnerable to loss
when we gather like this to one side,
around some death,

and try to weave it into our lives
—who can weave nothing but our ragged
routes across the desert.

And it is those among us
who most make the heavens their business
who go most deeply into this death-weaving.

As if the star might
spring from the dying mouth
or shoot from the agony of the eyes.

'We must not miss it,
however it comes.'
If it comes.

*

He stretched out his feet
and seemed to sink deeper in the bed,
and was still.

Sons no longer,
we pulled down his eyelids
and pushed the chin up gently to close his mouth,
and stood under the flapping roof.
Our shelter sheltered under the night.

*

Hides, furs and skins,
are our shelter and our garments.

We can weave nothing.

The Dispossessed

The lake is deserted now
but the water is still clean and transparent,
the headlands covered with laurels,
the little estuaries full of shells,
with enchanting parterres where the waves
ebb and flow over masses of turf and flowers.

It was like a miracle, a long pastoral, long ago.
The intoxication of a life gliding away
in the face of heaven: Spring,
a plain of flowers; Autumn, with grape-clusters
and chestnuts formed in its depths;
our warm nights passing under starlight.

We had established peace,
having learned to practise virtue
without expectation of recompense
—that we must be virtuous without hope.
(The Law is just; observe it,
maintain it, and it will bring contentment.)

Then, by the waterside, among the tortoises
with their mild and lively eyes, with crested larks
fluttering around Him, so light
they rested on a blade of grass
without bending it, He came among us
and lifted His unmangled hand:

These beauties, these earth-flowers growing and blowing,
what are they?
                    The spectacle of your humiliation!
If a man choose to enter the kingdom of peace
he shall not cease from struggle until he fail,
and having failed he will be astonished,
and having been astonished will rule,
and having ruled will rest.

Our dream curdled. We awoke
and began to thirst for the restoration of our house.
One morning, in a slow paroxysm of rage,
we found His corpse stretched on the threshold.

The Route of the Táin

Gene sat on a rock, dangling our map.
The others were gone over the next crest,
further astray. We ourselves, irritated,
were beginning to turn down toward the river
back to the car, the way we should have come.

We should have trusted our book.
After they tried a crossing, and this river too
'rose against them' and bore off
a hundred of their charioteers toward the sea
They had to move along the river Colptha
up to its source.
           There:
where the main branch sharpens away gloomily
to a gash in the hill opposite.

then to Bélat Ailiúin
                by that pathway
climbing back and forth out of the valley
over to Ravensdale.

Scattering in irritation. Who had set out
so cheerfully to celebrate our book;
cheerfully as we made and remade it
through a waste of hours, content to 'enrich the present
honouring the past', each to his own just function.
Wandering off, ill-sorted,
like any beasts of the field,
one snout honking disconsolate,
another burrowing in its pleasures.

When not far above us a red fox
ran at full stretch out of the bracken
and panted across the hillside toward the next ridge.
Where he vanished—a faint savage sharpness
out of the earth—an inlet of the sea
shone in the distance at the mouth of the valley
beyond Omeath: grey waters crawled with light.

For a heartbeat, in alien certainty,
we exchanged looks. We should have known it by now
—the process, the whole tedious enabling ritual.
Flux brought to fullness; saturated;
the clouding over; dissatisfaction
spreading slowly like an ache;
something reduced shivering suddenly
into meaning along new boundaries;

through a forest,
by a salt-dark shore,
by a standing stone on a dark plain,
by a ford running blood,
and along this gloomy pass, with someone ahead
calling and waving on the crest
against a heaven of dismantling cloud,
transfixed by the same figure (stopped, pointing)
on the rampart at Cruachan, where it began.

The morning sunlight pouring on us all
as we scattered over the mounds
disputing over useless old books,
assembled in cheerful speculation
around a prone block, *Miosgán Medba*
—Queen Medb's *turd* . . . ? And rattled our maps,
joking together in growing illness
or age or fat. Before us
the route of the *Táin*, over men's dust,
toward these hills that seemed to grow
darker as we drove nearer.

Ely Place

'Such a depth of charm here always . . .'

In Mortuary Lane a gull
cried on one of the Hospital gutters
I. I. I . . . harsh in sadness
on and on, beak and gullet
open against the blue.

Darkness poured down indoors
through a half light stale as the grave
over plates and silver bowls
glimmering on a side table.

Down at the corner a flicker of sex
—a white dress—against the railings.

'This is where George Moore . . .'

rasps

his phantom walking stick
without a sound, toward the Post Office
where her slight body, in white, has disappeared.

A blood vision started out of the brick:
a flustered perfumy dress;
a mothering shocked smile;
live muscle startling in skin.
The box of keys in my pocket
—I am opening it, tongue-tied.
I unpick the little penknife
and dig it in her throat,
in her spirting gullet.

And they are on it in a flash,
tongues of movement feeding,
ravenous and burrowing,
upstreaming through the sunlight with it
until it disappears, buried
in heaven, faint, far off.

'. . . with a wicked wit, but self-mocking;
and full of integrity behind it all . . .'

A few beginnings, a few
tentative tired endings
over and over.
                    Memoirs, maggots.
After lunch a quarter of an hour,
at most, of empty understanding.

Worker in Mirror, at his Bench

1

Silent rapt surfaces
assemble glittering
among themselves.

A few more pieces
What to call it . . .
                    Bright Assembly?
Foundations for a Tower?
Open Trap? Circular-Tending
Self-Reflecting Abstraction . . .

2

The shop doorbell rings.
A few people enter.

I am sorry. You have caught me
a little early in my preparations.

The way they mess with everything.
Smile. How they tighten their lips:
What *is* it about the man
that is so impossible to like?
The flashy coat, the flourished cuffs?
The ease under questioning . . .

Yes, everything is deliberate.
This floppy flower. Smile.
This old cutaway style—all the easier
to bare the breast. Comfortable smiles.
A cheap lapse—forgive me;
the temptation never sleeps.
The smiles more watery.

No, it has no practical application.
I am simply trying to understand something
—states of peace nursed out of wreckage.
The peace of fullness, not emptiness.

It is tedious, yes. The process is elaborate,
and wasteful—a dangerous litter
of lacerating pieces collects.
Let my rubbish stand witness.
Smile, stirring it idly with a shoe.

Take for example this work in hand.
Out of its waste matter
it should emerge solid and light.
One idea, grown with the thing itself,
should drive it searching inward
with a sort of life, due to the mirror effect.
Often, the more I simplify
the more a few simplicities
go burrowing in their own depths
until the guardian structure is aroused.

Most satisfying, yes.
Another kind of vigour, I agree
—unhappy until its actions are more convulsed:
the 'passionate'—might find it maddening.
Here the passion is in the putting together.

Yes, I suppose I am appalled
at the massiveness of others' work.
But not deterred. I have leaned my shed
against a solid wall. Understanding smiles.
I tinker with the things that dominate me
as they describe their random persistent coherences.
Clean surfaces shift and glitter among themselves.

Pause. We all are vile . . .
Let the voice die away.

Awkward silence
as they make their way out.

3

But they are right to be suspicious
when answers distract and conceal.
What is there to understand?
Time punishes—and this the flesh teaches.
Emptiness, is that not peace?

Conceal and permit: pursuit
at its most delicate, truth as tinkering,
easing the particular of its litter,
bending attention on the remaining depths
as though questions had never been.

He bends closer, testing the work.
The bright assembly begins to turn in silence.
The answering brain glitters—one system
answering another. The senses enter
and reach out with a pulse of pleasure
to the four corners of their own wilderness:

A gold mask, vast in the distance, stares back.
Familiar features. Naked sky-blue eyes.
(It is morning, once upon a time.)
Disappears. Was it a dream? Forgotten.

Reappears: enormous and wavering. Silver.
Stern and beautiful, with something
not yet pain in the eyes.
The forehead begins to wrinkle:
what ancient sweet time . . . Forgotten.

Reestablishes: a bronze head
thrown back across the firmament,
a bronze arm covering the eyes.
Pain established. Eyes
that have seen . . . Forgotten.

Dark as iron. All the light
hammered into two blazing eyes;
all the darkness into one wolf-muzzle.
Resist! An unholy tongue
laps brothers' thick blood.
Forget!

He straightens up, unseeing.

Did I dream another outline
in the silt of the sea floor?
Blunt stump of limb—a marble carcass
where no living thing can have crept,
below the last darkness, slowly,
as the earth ages, blurring with pressure.
The calm smile of a half-buried face:
eyeball blank, the stare inward
to the four corners of
what foul continuum.

Blackness—all matter
in one polished cliff face
hurtling rigid from zenith to pit
through dead

St Paul's Rocks: 16 February 1832

A cluster of rocks far from the trade routes,
a thousand miles from any other land,
they appear abruptly in the ocean,
low lying, so hidden in driving mists
they are seldom sighted, and then briefly,
white and glittering against the eternal grey.

Despite the lack of any vegetation
they have succeeded in establishing
symbiosis with the surrounding water.
Colonies of birds eat the abundant fish;
moths feed on the feathers; lice and beetles
live in the dung; countless spiders
prey on these scavengers; in the crevices
a race of crabs lives on the eggs and young.

In squalor and killing and parasitic things
life takes its first hold.
Later the noble accident: the seed,
dropped in some exhausted excrement,
or bobbing like a matted skull into an inlet.

Drowsing over The Arabian Nights

I nodded. The books agree,
one hopes for too much.
It is ridiculous.
We are elaborate beasts.

If we concur it is only
in our hunger: the soiled gullet.
And sleep's airy nothing.
And the moist matter of lust

—if the whole waste of women
could be gathered like one pit
under swarming Man,
then all might act together.

And the agonies of death,
as we enter our endless nights
quickly, one by one, fire
darting up to the roots of our hair.

Crab Orchard Sanctuary: Late October

The lake water lifted a little and fell
doped and dreamy in the late heat.
The air at lung temperature—like the end of the world:
a butterfly panted with dull scarlet wings
on the mud by the reeds, the tracks
of small animals softening along the edge,
a child's foot-prints, out too far.

The car park was empty. Long threads of spider silk
blew out softly from the tips of the trees.
A big spider stopped on the warm gravel,
sunlight charging the dark shell.

A naked Indian stepped out onto the grass
silent and savage, faded,
grew transparent, disappeared.

A speedboat glistened slowly in the distance.
A column of smoke climbed from the opposite shore.
In the far inlets clouds of geese flew about
quarrelling and settling in.

*

                                        That morning
two thin quails appeared in our garden
stepping one by one with piping movements
across the grass, feeding. I watched a long time
until they rounded the corner of the house.
A few grey wasps still floated about at the eaves;
crickets still chirruped in the grass
—but in growing silence—after last week's frosts.
Now a few vacated bodies, locust wraiths,
light as dry scale, begin to drift
on the driveway among the leaves,
stiff little Fuseli devil bodies.
Hidden everywhere, a myriad
leather seed-cases lie in wait
nourishing curled worms of white fat
—ugly, in absolute certainty, piteous,
threatening in every rustling sound:
bushes worrying in the night breeze,
dry leaves detaching, and creeping.
They will swarm again, on suffocated nights,
with their endless hysterics; and wither away again.

*

Who will stand still then, listening
to that woodpecker knocking, and watch
the erratic jays and cardinals flashing
blue and red among the branches and trunks;
that bronze phantom pausing; and this . . . stock-still,
with glittering brain, withering away.

It is an ending already.
The road hot and empty, taken over
by spiders, and pairs of butterflies twirling
about one another, and grasshoppers leap-
drifting over the gravel, birds darting
fluttering through the heat.
                                        What solitary step.

A slow hot glare out on the lake
spreading over the water.

Wyncote, Pennsylvania: a gloss

A mocking-bird on a branch
outside the window, where I write,
gulps down a wet crimson berry,
shakes off a few bright drops
from his wing, and is gone
into a thundery sky.

Another storm coming.
Under that copper light
my papers seem luminous.
And over them I will take
ever more painstaking care.

PEPPERCANISTER POEMS

BUTCHER'S DOZEN (1972)

I went with Anger at my heel
Through Bogside of the bitter zeal
—Jesus pity!—on a day
Of cold and drizzle and decay.
A month had passed. Yet here remained
A murder smell that stung and stained.
On flats and alleys—over all—
It hung; on battered roof and wall,
On wreck and rubbish scattered thick,
On sullen steps and pitted brick.
And when I came where thirteen died
It shrivelled up my heart. I sighed
And looked about that brutal place
Of rage and terror and disgrace.
Then my moistened lips grew dry.
I had heard an answering sigh!
There in a ghostly pool of blood
A crumpled phantom hugged the mud:
'Once there lived a hooligan.
A pig came up, and away he ran.
Here lies one in blood and bones,
Who lost his life for throwing stones.'
More voices rose. I turned and saw
Three corpses forming, red and raw,
From dirt and stone. Each upturned face
Stared unseeing from its place:
'Behind this barrier, blighters three,
We scrambled back and made to flee.
The guns cried *Stop*, and here lie we.'
Then from left and right they came,
More mangled corpses, bleeding, lame,
Holding their wounds. They chose their ground,
Ghost by ghost, without a sound,
And one stepped forward, soiled and white:
'A bomber I. I travelled light
—Four pounds of nails and gelignite
About my person, hid so well
They seemed to vanish where I fell.

When the bullet stopped my breath
A doctor sought the cause of death.
He upped my shirt, undid my fly,
Twice he moved my limbs awry,
And noticed nothing. By and by
A soldier, with his sharper eye,
Beheld the four elusive rockets
Stuffed in my coat and trouser pockets.
Yes, they must be strict with us,
Even in death so treacherous!'
He faded, and another said:
'We three met close when we were dead.
Into an armoured car they piled us
Where our mingled blood defiled us,
Certain, if not dead before,
To suffocate upon the floor.
Careful bullets in the back
Stopped our terrorist attack,
And so three dangerous lives are done
—Judged, condemned and shamed in one.'
That spectre faded in his turn.
A harsher stirred, and spoke in scorn:
'The shame is theirs, in word and deed,
Who prate of Justice, practise greed,
And act in ignorant fury—then,
Officers and gentlemen,
Send to their Courts for the Most High
To tell us did we really die.
Does it need recourse to law
To tell ten thousand what they saw?
The news is out. The troops were kind.
Impartial justice has to find
We'd be alive and well today
If we had let them have their way.
But friend and stranger, bride and brother,
Son and sister, father, mother,
All not blinded by your smoke,
Photographers who caught your stroke,

The priests that blessed our bodies, spoke
And wagged our blood in the world's face.
The truth will out, to your disgrace.'
He flushed and faded. Pale and grim,
A joking spectre followed him:
'Take a bunch of stunted shoots,
A tangle of transplanted roots,
Ropes and rifles, feathered nests,
Some dried colonial interests,
A hard unnatural union grown
In a bed of blood and bone,
Tongue of serpent, gut of hog
Spiced with spleen of underdog.
Stir in, with oaths of loyalty,
Sectarian supremacy,
And heat, to make a proper botch,
In a bouillon of bitter Scotch.
Last, the choice ingredient: you.
Now, to crown your Irish stew,
Boil it over, make a mess.
A most imperial success!'
He capered weakly, racked with pain,
His dead hair plastered in the rain:
The group was silent once again.
It seemed the moment to explain
That sympathetic politicians
Say our violent traditions,
Backward looks and bitterness
Keep us in this dire distress.
We must forget, and look ahead,
Nurse the living, not the dead.
My words died out. A phantom said:
'Here lies one who breathed his last
Firmly reminded of the past.
A trooper did it, on one knee,
In tones of brute authority.'
That harsher spirit, who before
Had flushed with anger, spoke once more:
'Simple lessons cut most deep.

This lesson in our hearts we keep:
You condescend to hear us speak
Only when we slap your cheek.
And yet we lack the last technique:
We rap for order with a gun,
The issues simplify to one
—Then your Democracy insists
You mustn't talk with terrorists.
White and yellow, black and blue,
Have learned their history from you:
Divide and ruin, muddle through,
We speak in wounds. Behold this mess.
My curse upon your politesse.'
Another ghost stood forth, and wet
Dead lips that had not spoken yet:
'My curse on the cunning and the bland,
On gentlemen who loot a land
They do not care to understand;
Who keep the natives on their paws
With ready lash and rotten laws;
Then if the beasts erupt in rage
Give them a slightly larger cage
And, in scorn and fear combined,
Turn them against their own kind.
The game runs out of room at last,
A people rises from its past,
The going gets unduly tough
And you have, surely, had enough.
The time has come to yield your place
With condescending show of grace
—An Empire-builder handing on.
We reap the ruin when you've gone,
All your errors heaped behind you:
Promises that do not bind you,
Hopes in conflict, cramped commissions,
Faiths exploited, and traditions.'
Bloody sputum filled his throat.
He stopped and coughed to clear it out,
And finished, with his eyes a-glow:

140

'You came, you saw, you conquered . . . So.
You gorged—and it was time to go.
Good riddance. We'd forget—released—
But for the rubbish of your feast,
The slops and scraps that fell to earth
And sprang to arms in dragon birth.
Sashed and bowler-hatted, glum
Apprentices of fife and drum,
High and dry, abandoned guards
Of dismal streets and empty yards,
Drilled at the codeword "True Religion"
To strut and mutter like a pigeon
"Not An Inch—Up The Queen";
Who use their walls like a latrine
For scribbled magic—at their call,
Straight from the nearest music-hall,
Pope and Devil intertwine,
Two cardboard kings appear, and join
In one more battle by the Boyne!
Who could love them? God above . . .'
'Yet pity is akin to love,'
The thirteenth corpse beside him said,
Smiling in its bloody head,
'And though there's reason for alarm
In dourness and a lack of charm
Their cursed plight calls out for patience.
They, even they, with other nations
Have a place, if we can find it.
Love our changeling! Guard and mind it.
Doomed from birth, a cursed heir,
Theirs is the hardest lot to bear,
Yet not impossible, I swear,
If England would but clear the air
And brood at home on her disgrace
—Everything to its own place.
Face their walls of dole and fear
And be of reasonable cheer.
Good men every day inherit
Father's foulness with the spirit,

Purge the filth and do not stir it.
Let them out. At least let in
A breath or two of oxygen,
So they may settle down for good
And mix themselves in the common blood.
We all are what we are, and that
Is mongrel pure. What nation's not
Where any stranger hung his hat
And seized a lover where she sat?'
He ceased and faded. Zephyr blew
And all the others faded too.
I stood like a ghost. My fingers strayed
Along the fatal barricade.
The gentle rainfall drifting down
Over Colmcille's town
Could not refresh, only distil
In silent grief from hill to hill.

A SELECTED LIFE (1972)

1 *Galloping Green: May 1962*

He clutched the shallow drum
and crouched forward, thin
as a beast of prey. The shirt
stretched at his waist. He stared
to one side, toward the others,
and struck the skin cruelly
with his nails. Sharp
as the answering arid bark
his head quivered, counting.

2 *Coolea: 6 October 1971*

A fine drizzle blew
softly across the tattered valley
onto my glasses, and covered
my mourning suit with tiny drops.

A crow scuffled in the hedge
and floated out with a dark groan
into full view. It flapped up the field
and lit on a rock, and scraped its beak.
It croaked: a voice out of the rock
carrying across the slope. Foretell.

Foretell: the Sullane river winding downward
in darker green through the fields
and disappearing behind his house;
cars parking in the lane; a bare yard;
family and friends collecting in the kitchen;
a shelf there, concertinas sprawled in the dust,
the pipes folded on their bag.
The hole waiting in the next valley.
That.

A rat lay on its side in the wet,
the grey skin washed clean and fleshy,
the little face wrinkled back in hatred,
the back torn open. A pale string
stretched on the gravel. Devil-martyr:
your sad, mad meat.
                              I have interrupted
some thing . . . You! Croaking
on your wet stone. Flesh picker.

The drizzle came thick and fast suddenly.
Down in the village the funeral bell began to beat.

*

And you. Waiting in the dark chapel.
Packed and ready. Upon your hour.
Leaving . . . A few essentials forgotten

—a standard array of dependent beings,
small, smaller, pale, paler, in black;

—sundry musical effects: a piercing
sweet consort of whistles crying,
goosenecked wail and yelp of pipes,
melodeons snoring in sadness,
drum bark, the stricken
harpsichord's soft crash;

—a lurid cabinet: fire's flames
plotting in the dark; hugger mugger
and murder; collapsing back in laughter.
Angry goblets of Ireland's tears,
stuffed with fire, touch. Salut!
Men's guts ignite and whiten in satisfaction;

—a workroom, askew: fumbling at the table
tittering, pools of idea forming.
A contralto fills the room
with Earth's autumnal angst; the pools coalesce.

Here and there in the shallows dim spirits
glide, poissons de la melancolie.
The banks above are smothered in roses;
among their glowing harmonies, bathed in charm,
a cavalier returns in fancy dress,
embracing her loving prize; two baby angels,
each holding a tasseled curtain-corner,
flutter down, clucking and mocking complacently.
Liquids of romance, babbling
on the concrete floor. Let us draw a veil.

3 *St Gobnait's Graveyard, Ballyvourney: that evening*

The gate creaked in the dusk. The trampled grass,
soaked and still, was disentangling
among the standing stones
after the day's excess.

A flock of crows circled
the church tower, scattered
and dissolved chattering
into the trees. Fed.

His first buried night
drew on. Unshuddering.
And welcome.
Shudder for him,

Pierrot limping forward in the sun
out of Merrion Square, long ago,
in black overcoat and beret,
pale as death from his soiled bed,

swallowed back: animus
brewed in clay, uttered
in brief meat and brains, flattened
back under our flowers.

Gold and still he lay,
on his secondlast bed. *Dottore!* A withered smile,
the wry hands lifted. *A little while
and you may not.*

Salut.
Slán.
Yob tvoyu mat'.
Master, your health.

VERTICAL MAN (1973)

4 *Philadelphia: 3 October 1972*

I was pouring a drink when the night-monotony
was startled below by a sudden howling
of engines along Market Street,
curséd ambulances intermixing their screams
down the dark canyons.

Over the gramophone your death-mask
was suddenly awake
and I felt something of you
out in the night, near and moving nearer,
tittering, uneasy.

I thought we had laid you to rest
—that you had been directed toward
crumbling silence, and the like.
It seems it is hard to keep
a vertical man down.

I lifted the glass, and the furies
redoubled their distant screams.
To you: the bourbon-breath.
To me, for the time being,
the real thing.

'There has grown lately upon the soul
a covering as of earth and stone,
thick and rough . . .'
                    I had been remembering
the sour ancient phrases . . .
                              'Very well,
seemingly the argument requires it:
let us assume mankind is worth considering . . .'

That particular heaviness.
                              That the days pass,
that our tasks arise, dominate our energies,
are mastered with difficulty and some pleasure,
and are obsolete. That there can be a sweet stir
hurrying in the veins (earned: this sunlight
—this oxygen—are my *reward*) and the ground
grows dull to the tread. The ugly rack: let it ride.
That you may startle the heart of a whole people
(as you know) and all your power,
with its delicate, self-mocking adjustments,
is soon beating to a coarse pulse
to glut fantasy and sentiment.
That for all you have done, the next beginning
is as lonely, as random, as gauche and unready,
as presumptuous, as the first,
when you stripped and advanced timidly
toward nothing in particular.
Though with a difference—there is
a kind of residue. Not an increase in weight
(we must not become portly; your admired D******,
the lush intellectual glamour loosening
to reveal the travelogue beneath).
But a residue in the timidity,
a maturer unsureness, as we
prepare to undergo preparatory error.

Only this morning . . . that desultory moment or two
standing at the rain-stained glass; a while more
looking over the charts pinned on the wall;
to sit down with the folder of notes on the left
and clean paper on the right, the pen beside it,
and remove and put down the spectacles and bury
my face in my hands, in self-devouring prayer,
till the charts and notes come crawling to life again
under a Night seething with
soft incandescent bombardment!

At the dark zenith a pulse beat,
a sperm of light separated wriggling
and snaked in a slow beam down
the curve of the sky, through faint
structures and hierarchies
of elements and things and beasts. It fell,
a packed star, dividing
and redividing until it was
a multiple gold tear. It dropped
toward the horizon, entered
bright Quincunx newly risen,
beat with a blinding flame and dis-
appeared. I stared, duly blinded.
An image burned on the brain
—a woman-animal: scaled,
pierced in paws and heart,
ecstatically calm. It faded
to a far-off desolate call,

> a child's.

If the eye could follow that, accustomed to
that dark.

> But that is your domain.

At which thought, your presence
turned back toward the night.

> (*Wohin* . . .)
>
> Stay

a while. Since you are here.

> At least

we have *Das Lied von der Erde*
and a decent record-player together
at the one place and time.

> With a contraction

of the flesh . . . A year exactly since you died!

I arrested the needle. The room filled
with a great sigh. In terror and memory
I lowered the tiny point toward our youth
—into those bright cascades!
                              Radiant outcry—
trumpets and drenching strings—exultant tenor—
Schadenfreude! The waste!
                              Abject. Irrecoverable.

*

The golden bourbon winks in the glass. For the road.
But wait, there is something I must show you first,
a song of cark and care. A drinking—a *drunken*—song
for the misery of this world . . . Not quite right yet
—but very soulful. To give you a hollow laugh.

> Let Gloom gather, and deject
>   the soul's gardens.
> Let Joy shrivel up and die
>   and song with it.
> For Life is a black business.
>   While as for Death—
>
> Therefore, a little music, a little something
>   —a timely tumbler.
> Earth has not anything
>   to show more fair,
> Life being what it is.
>   And as for Death—
>
> The azure firmament
>   is permanent.
> The Earth is here to stay
>   and always good
> for another Primavera.
>   Whereas Man—

Would you care to share a queer vision I had?
By your gravestone . . .
                        It was moonlight.
And there was something crouching there—ape-shaped!—
demented, howling out
silent foulness, accurséd silent screams
into the fragrant Night.

*

The golden goodness trembles. It is time.
And more than time. Kindly step forward.
A black bloody business,
                        the whole thing.

He stepped forward through the cigarette-smoke
to his place at the piano
—all irritation—and tore
off his long fingernails to play.

From palatal darkness a voice
rose flickering, and checked
in glottal silence. The song
articulated and pierced.

We leaned over the shallows from the boat slip
and netted the little grey shrimp-ghosts
snapping, and dropped them
in the crawling biscuit-tin.

THE GOOD FIGHT (1973)

A Poem for the 10th Anniversary of the Death of John F. Kennedy

In 1962 people began seriously to calculate that, if the three brothers took the Presidency in succession, it would carry the country to 1984 . . . the succession could then pass to the sons.—Henry Fairlie, *The Kennedy Promise* (1973)

Those who are imprisoned in the silence of reality always use a gun (or, if they are more fortunate, a pen) to speak for them—John Clellon Holmes, 'The Silence of Oswald', *Playboy* (November 1965)

1

Once upon a time a certain phantom
took to certain red-smelling corridors
in sore need. It met, with a flush of pleasure,
the smell of seed and swallowed
life and doom in the same animal action.

(Mere substance—our métier.
This is our nature, the human mouth
tasting Justice or a favourite soup
with equal relish.)

             He wiped his lips
and leaned tiredly against the window,
flying through the night. The darkened cabin
creaked under a few weak blue lights.
Outside, half seen, the fields of stars
chilled his forehead, their millions centred on
the navigator.
             Not commanding. Steering.

*Can we believe it possible for anyone
to master the art of steering while he must
at the same time expend his best skill
gaining control of the helm?*

                                        His hands flexed.
All reasonable things are possible.

All that day, the reporters in the corridor
had pushed closer to the room.
As the hours passed, the press of human beings
—the sweat and smoke—built up
a meaty odour.

Once, he rolled up his sleeve
and looked at the calloused, scratched arm:
'Ohio did that to me.'
(One day in Philadelphia
his hand *burst* with blood.)

He rolled the sleeve down again
and shook his head, not understanding,
then became cool again as ever,
asking: 'Who made that decision?
Who had command decision then?'

*

Shock-headed, light-footed, he swung
an invisible cloak about him in the uproar
and hunched down from the platform at them,
his hands in his jacket pockets.
A jugular pleasure beat in his throat.

'Ever free and strong
we will march along, going to meet
the harsh bright demands of the West, building
a new City on a New Frontier,
where led and leader bend their wills together
in necessary rule—admit
no limit but the possible, grant
to each endeavour its appointed post,
its opportunity to serve:

our Youth carrying its ideals
into the fettered places of the earth;
our Strength on guard at every door of freedom
around the world; our Art and Music
down from the dark garret—into the sun!
The eyes of the world upon us!'

He held out his inflamed right hand
for the Jaw to grip. The sinews winced.
Crude hand-lettered signs danced in the murk.

'Forward, then, in higher urgency,
adventuring with risk,
raising each other to our moral best,
aspiring to the sublime
in warlike simplicity, our power
justified upon our excellence!

If other nations falter
their people still remain what they were.
But if our country in its call to greatness
falters, we are little but the scum
of other lands. That is our special danger,
our burden and our glory.
The accident that brought our people together
out of blind necessities
—embrace it!—explosive—to our bodies.'

(It sounds as though it could go on for ever,
yet there is a shape to it—Appropriate
Performance. Another almost perfect
working model. But it gets harder.
The concepts jerk and wrestle, back to back.

The finer the idea the harder it is
to assemble lifelike. It adopts hardnesses
and inflexibilities, knots, impossible joints
made possible only by stress,
and good for very little afterward.)

'Welcome challenge, that can stretch
the two sinews of the Soul,
Body and Mind, to a pure pitch,
so we may strike the just note
inside and out . . .'

                              'Peace—a process,
a way of solving problems . . .'

                                        'Leisure—
an opportunity to perfect
those things of which we now despair . . .'

'—Let us make ourselves vessels of decision!
We are not here to curse the darkness.
The old order changes! Men
firm in purpose and clear in thought
channel by their own decisions
forces greater than any man!'

The swaying mass exclaimed
about the great
dream
            steps . . .

(Where is a young man's heart in such a scene?
Who would not be stunned by the beast's opinion?
Nor think wisdom control of the beast's moods?
What schooling will resist, and not be swamped
and swept downstream? What can a young man do?
Especially if he belong to a great city
and be one of her rich and noble citizens
and also fine to look upon, and tall?)

He turned to go, murmuring aside
with a boyish grin:
                              'If anybody calls
say I am
raping the intellectuals.'

Inside, a group of specialists,
chosen for their incomparable dash,
were gathered around
a map of the world's regions
with all kinds of precision instruments.

2

A lonely room.
            An electric fire
glowing in one corner. He is lying on his side.
It is late. He is at the centre of a city,
awake.

          Above and below him
there are other rooms, with others in them.
He knows nobody as yet, and has
no wish to. Outside the window
the street noises ascend.

His cell hangs in the night.

He could give up.
But there is something he must do.

And though the night passes, and the morning
brings back familiarity, and he goes out
about his business as though nothing had changed
—energyless at his assigned tasks—
and though the evening comes and he discovers
for the first time where to buy bread and tomatoes,
milk and meat, and climbs the dirty stairs
and takes possession for the second time,
and soon discovers how to light the gas
and where to put things, and where to sit
so he can read and eat at the same time,
and reads a long time
with the crumbs hardening and a tawny scum
shrinking on the cold tea, and finally
ventures out for his first night prowl
and takes possession of his neighbourhood,

learning at each turn, and turns for home,
and takes possession for the third time,
and reads, and later settles to sleep; and though
next morning he wakes up to a *routine*
for the first time, and goes to work,
repeats his necessary purchases
and manages the routine a little better,
with a less conscious effort; and night begins
to bring familiarity, and finds him
beginning to think at last
of what he is here for; and night follows night
and on a certain evening he puts aside
his cup and plate, and draws his journal to him
and revolves his pen meditatively.

I cannot reach or touch anything.
I cannot lay my hand with normal weight
on anything. It is either nothing
or too much.
                    I have stood out
in the black rain and waited
and concentrated among
those over-lit ruins
irritable and hungry
and not known what city.

I have glided in loveless dream transit
over the shadowy sea floor,
satisfied in the knowledge
that if I once slacken in my savagery
I will drown.

I have watched my own
theatrical eyes narrow
and noted under what stress
and ceaseless changes of mind.
I have seen very few
cut so dull and driven a figure,
masked in scorn or abrupt
impulse, knowing content
nowhere.

And I have forgotten
what rain and why I waited
what city from room to room
forgotten with father.
                              But not
what hunger as I move
toward some far sum-total,
attacked under others' eyes.

I have seen myself, a 'thing'
in my own eyes, lifting
my hand empty and opening
and closing my mouth
in senseless mimicry
and wondered why I am alive
or why a man can live in this way.

I believed once that silence
encloses each one of us.
Now, if that silence does not
enclose *each*, as I am led
more and more to understand
—so that I truly am cut off,
a 'thing' in their eyes also—
I can, if my daydreams are right,
decide to end it.

Soak left wrist in cold water
to numb the pain.
Then slash my wrist and plunge it
into bathtub of hot water.
Somewhere, a violin plays,
as I watch my life whirl away.
I think to myself 'How easy to Die'
and 'A Sweet Death' (to violins).

Or I might reach out and touch.
And he would turn this way
inquiring—Who was that!
What decision was this . . .

	An ambitious man, in a city
and not justice?	*where honour is the dominant*
	principle, is soon broken upon the
	city as a ship is broken on a
	reef.

*Passion, ignorance and concupis-
cence are obscurities clouding
the soul's natural judgement. They
are the origin of crime.*

	There is none so small or so high
	but that he shall pay the fitting
	penalty, either in this world or in
yet more savage!	*some yet more savage place*
conveyed!	*whither he shall be conveyed . . .*

*Great crimes, that sink into the
abyss . . .*

*Images of evil in a foul
pasture . . .*

	—There are those,
	lower still, that seat Greed and
	Money on their throne, and make
squat!	*Reason and the Spirit squat on*
	the floor under it . . .

*—Democracy cries out for
Tyranny; and the Tyrant becomes
a wolf instead of a man . . .*

The rest! The whole	*—The rest damned to a constant*
world but one! An	*flux of pain and pleasure. They*
impossible	*struggle greedily for their*
logic-being	*pleasures, and butt and kick with*
	horns and hoofs of iron.

<pre>
        man   beast

    (d)amn

                    best

        mean
                      r i
        team   b a n s
                     ⋏   ⋏

        meat
</pre>

I wonder what would happen if somebody was to stand up and say
he was utterly opposed not only to the government but to the
people, to the entire land and complete foundations of his society?

3

She was humming to herself
among the heavy-scented magnolia bowers,
chic, with shining eyes, smiling at
Power and its attendant graces,
Aphrodite in Washington,

when all of a sudden a black
shadow or a black ruin
or a cliff of black
crossed at rigid speed
and spoiled everything.

Everybody started throwing themselves down
and picking themselves up and running
around the streets looking in each other's face
and saying 'Catastrophe' and weeping
and saying 'Well! That's that.'

For a few days great numbers of people
couldn't sleep, and lost appetite. Children experienced
alarm at the sight of their parents crying.
There were many who admitted
they expected the President's ghost to appear.

Various forms of castration dreads emerged,
probably out of fear of retribution
for unconscious parricidal wishes.
Anxiety was widespread, with apprehension
of worse things to come.

It was unhealthy—a distortion of normal attitudes.
Things had been exalted
altogether out of proportion. Afterward,
when the shock was over, matters settled down
with surprising swiftness, almost with relief:

shudder
and return
            —a fish, flung back,
that lay stunned, shuddered into consciousness,
then dived back into the depths.

And somewhere in some laughable echo-chamber, for ever,
a prayer came snarling through devilish electrical smoke,
and, blinded by the light reflecting from
the snow everywhere, Dr Frost tottered forward
scratching his head, and opening his mouth:

4

I am in disarray. Maybe if I
were to fumble through my papers again.
I can no longer, in the face of so much
—so much . . .
            It is very hard.

But there is nothing for it. On this
everything in me is agreed.

So, weak a thousand ways,
I have come, I have made toward this place,
among wells of profound energy
and monuments to power and tedium.
Not in judgement, and not
in acceptance either.
                              Uncertain.
For if all you wish to do
is curse the world and your place in it
—well then . . .
                              But some appetite
is not satisfied
with that, is dissatisfied unless—

The manipulation, the special pleading,
the cross-weaving of these
'vessels of decision',
the one so 'heroic',
the other so . . .
                              You have to
wear them down against each other
to get any purchase,
and then there is this
strain.
                    That all *un*reasonable things
are possible. *Everything*
that can happen will happen.

My brothers, huddled in wait,
feeble warriors, self-chosen,
in our secondary world . . .
—who can't take our eyes off anything;
who harp on Love and Art and Truth too often:
it is appropriate for us
to proceed now and make our attempts
in private, to shuffle off and disappoint
Plato.

      (His 'philosophic nature'
—balance, you will remember;
apportionment, as between Mind and Body!
Harmony, and proper pitch!
The Dance!)

            Plump and faithless;
cut, as it were, in the sinews
of our souls; each other's worst company;
it is we, letting things *be*,
who might come at understanding.
That is the source of our patience.
Reliable first in the direction
and finally in the particulars of our response,
fumbling from doubt to doubt,
one day we might knock
our papers together, and elevate them
(with a certain self-abasement)
—their gleaming razors
mirroring a primary world
where power also is a source of patience
for a while before the just flesh
falls back in black dissolution in its box.

ONE (1974)

Prologue
*The storyteller's face
turned toward the fire.
He honed his flickering blade.*

*The sun tunnelled onward
eating into the universe's thin dusts
with the World waltzing after it*

*—Bith, a planetary pearl-blue
flushed with sheets of light,
signed with a thin white wake,*

the Voyage of the First Kindred

*Up and awake. Up straight
in absolute hunger
out of this black lair, and eat!*

*Driven rustling blind over
fragments of old frights and furies,
then with a sudden hiss into
a grey sheen of light. A pale space
everywhere alive with bits and pieces,
little hearts beating in their
furryfeathery bundles, transfixed.*

*That. There.
Hurling toward it, whimswift.
Snapdelicious. So necessary.
Another. Throbflutter. Swallowed.
And another.
The ache . . . The ease!
And another.*

But with the satisfaction
comes a falling off
in the drive, the desire.
The two energies approach and come to terms,
balance somehow, grow still.

Afterward I dreamed that I was sprawled out
winding across the heavens.
The first part of my dream was dominated
by thrashing wings, a gaping beak
—some natural threat out of the void.
I associate this, in its origins,
with the difficulties of digestion,
in its circumstantial detail
with an awareness (not amounting to guilt)
of the many little sufferers involved.

I passed the second and deeper part passively,
supported, captive, in a cosmic grip.
It seemed timeless, but during this period
my body aged, the skin loosened.
I associate this with the process of absorption.

In the third part of the dream I saw
—I was—two discs of light in the heavens
trembling in momentary balance.
They started to part. There would be a pang, I knew.
I associate this with the return of hunger.

During the last part I am coiled in combat
with giant particular forces among the stars,
writhing to escape. I manage it
in a final spasm, leaving my decrepit skin
clutched in fierce hands, and plunge downward,
fragments falling after me through space.

Down! Like a young thing!
Coil, now, and wait.
Sleep on these things.

The Entire Fabric

Shortly before the first hour,
at dead of night, a wave of cold
came from below, the Shades stirred
in their noble chairs. The stage before them
lightened and discovered dirt,
a neglected pavement, an ivied corner
with metal gates and temple pillars
—a mean backdrop: a broad street
with boarded windows and scribbled walls.
Down against the temple steps
a metal grating set in the floor
creaked open, emitting first
a puff of some contrived fumes
fitful with theatrical fire,
then a pinkish glitter of chrome.
A tableau rattled up from the crypt:
a man, sporting a striped jacket,
posed in confident quackery, bearded;
a woman, drawn up like a queen,
rouged and spangled. A round pot
bubbled on a stand between them
leaking a phosphorescent mist.
The lift stopped. Something flashed
in his right hand as he reached out
to touch the vessel's rim, once.
Faint strains of music stole
out of the fumes, and filled the air
—the entire fabric sang softly.
He paced forward. A spotlight struck:
he peered in mock intensity,
a hand cupped behind an ear,
out at the waiting dark, as if
searching the distance. He made to speak.
Above the temple, in the flies,
a mechanism began to whirr.

Finistère

1
One.

I smelt the weird Atlantic.
Finistère . . .
              Finisterre . . .

The sea surface darkened. The land behind me,
and all its cells and cists, grew dark.
From a bald boulder on the cairn top
I spied out the horizon to the northwest
and sensed that minute imperfection again.
Where the last sunken ray withdrew.
A point of light.

A maggot of the possible
wriggled out of the spine
into the brain.

We hesitated before that wider sea
but our heads sang with purpose
and predatory peace.

And whose excited blood was that
fumbling our movements? Whose ghostly hunger
tunneling our thoughts full of passages
smelling of death and clay and faint metals
and great stones in the darkness?

At no great distance out in the bay
the swell took us into its mercy,
grey upheaving slopes of water
sliding under us, collapsing,
crawling onward, mountainous.

Driven outward a day and a night
we held fast, numbed by the steady
might of the oceanic wind.
We drew close together, as one,
and turned inward, salt chaos
rolling in silence all around us,
and listened to our own mouths
mumbling in the sting of spray:
      —Ill wind end well
      mild mother
      on wild water pour peace

      who gave us our unrest
      whom we meet and unmeet
      in whose yearning shadow
      we erect our great uprights
      and settle fulfilled
      and build and are still
      unsettled, whose goggle gaze
      and holy howl we have scraped
      speechless on slabs of stone
      poolspirals opening on
      closing spiralpools
      and dances drilled in the rock
      in coil zigzag angle and curl
      river ripple earth ramp
      suncircle moonloop . . .
      in whose outflung service
      we nourished our hunger
      uprooted and came
      in whale hell
                gale gullet
   salt hole
                dark nowhere
   calm queen
                pour peace

The bad dream ended at last.
In the morning, in a sunny breeze,
bare headlands rose fresh out of the waves.
We entered a deep bay, lying open
to all the currents of the ocean.
We were further than anyone had ever been
and light-headed with exhaustion and relief
—three times we misjudged and were nearly driven
on the same rock.
                 (I had felt all this before.)
We steered in along a wall of mountain
and entered a quiet hall of rock echoing
to the wave-wash and our low voices.
I stood at the prow. We edged to a slope of stone.

I steadied myself. 'Our Father. . .' someone said
and there was a little laughter. I stood
searching a moment for the right words.
They fell silent. I chose the old words once more
and stepped out. At the solid shock
a dreamy power loosened at the base of my spine
and uncoiled and slid up through the marrow.
A flow of seawater over the rock fell back
with a she-hiss, plucking at my heel.
My tongue stumbled

Who
    is a breath
that makes the wind
that makes the wave
that makes this voice?

Who
    is the bull with seven scars
the hawk on the cliff
the salmon sunk in his pool
the pool sunk in her soil
the animal's fury

the flower's fibre
a teardrop in the sun?

Who
    is the word that spoken
the spear springs
    and pours out terror
the spark springs
    and burns in the brain?

When men meet on the hill
dumb as stones in the dark
    (the craft knocked behind me)
who is the jack of all light?
Who goes in full into
the moon's interesting conditions?
Who fingers the sun's sink hole:
    (I went forward, reaching out)

The Oldest Place

We approached the shore. Once more.
                              Repeated memory
shifted among the green-necked confused waves.
The sea wind and spray tugged and refreshed us,
but the stale reminder of our sin still clung.

We would need to dislodge
the flesh itself, to dislodge that
—shrivel back to the first drop
and be spat back shivering into
the dark beyond our first father.

*

We fished and fowled and chopped at the forest,
cooked and built, ploughed and planted,
danced and drank, all as before.
But worked inland, and got further.

And there was something in the way the land behaved:
passive, but responding. It grew under our hands.
We worked it like a dough to our requirements
yet it surprised us more than once
with a firm life of its own, as if it
used us.
　　　　　Once, as we were burying
one of our children, the half-dug grave
dampened, and overbrimmed, and the water
ran out over the land and would not stop
until the place had become a lake.

*

Year followed year.
The first skin blemishes appeared,
and it almost seemed we had been waiting for them.
The sickness and the dying began again.

To make things easier, we decided
to come together in one place.
We thought of the bare plain we found first,
with the standing stone: miles of dead clay
without a trace of a root or a living thing.
We gathered there and the sick died
and we covered them. Others fell sick
and we covered them, fewer and fewer.
A day came when I fell down by the great stone
alone, crying, at the middle of the stinking plain.

*

Night fell, and I lay there face down,
and I dreamed that my ghost stood up
and faint starry shadows everywhere
lifted themselves up and began
searching about among themselves for something,
hesitant at first, but quickly certain,
and all turning

                        —muscular nothingnesses,
demons, animal-heads, wrestling vaguely toward me
reaching out terrible gifts into my face,
clawfuls of dripping cloth
and gold and silver things.
They passed through me . . .

                        To the stone,
and draped it with their gifts, murmuring,
and dropped them about its base.
With each gift, the giver
sighed and melted away,
the black stone packed more
with dark radiance.

                        And I dreamed
that my ghost moved toward it, hand on heart,
the other hand advanced.
                        And its glare
gathered like a pulse, and struck
on the withered plain of my own brain.

*

A draped black shaft under the starlight,
with bars and blocks and coils of restless metal
piled about it, and eyes hovering
above those abnormal stirrings.
A little higher, where there might have been branches,
a complex emptiness shimmered in front of the stars.

A shawl shifted on the top, dangled
black and silver, a crumpled face
with forehead torn crisscross, begging,
with tongue flapping,
and dropped to earth.

38 Phoenix Street

Look.
> I was lifted up
past rotten bricks weeds
to look over the wall.
A mammy lifted up a baby on the other side.
Dusty smells. Cat. Flower bells
hanging down purple red.

Look.
> The other. Looking.
My finger picked at a bit of dirt
on top of the wall and a quick
wiry redgolden thing
ran back down a little hole.

*

We knelt up on our chairs in the lamplight
and leaned on the brown plush, watching the gramophone.
The turning record shone and hissed
under the needle, liftfalling, liftfalling.
John McCormack chattered in his box.

Two little tongues of flame burned
in the lamp chimney, wavering
their tips. On the glassy belly
little drawnout images quivered.
Jimmy's mammy was drying the delph in the shadows.

*

Mister Cummins always hunched down
sad and still beside the stove,
with his face turned away toward the bars.
His mouth so calm, and always set so sadly.
A black rubbery scar stuck on his white forehead.

Sealed in his sad cave. Hisshorror erecting
slowly out of its rock nests, nosing the air.
He was buried for three days under a hill of dead,
the faces congested down all round him
grinning *Dardanelles!* in the dark.

They noticed him by a thread of blood
glistening among the black crusts on his forehead.
His heart gathered all its weakness, to beat.

A worm hanging down, its little round
black mouth open. Sad father.

*

I spent the night there once
in a strange room, tucked in against the wallpaper
on the other side of our own bedroom wall.

Up in a corner of the darkness the Sacred Heart
leaned down in his long clothes over a red oil lamp
with his women's black hair and his eyes lit up in red,
hurt and blaming. He held out the Heart
with his women's fingers, like a toy.

The lamp-wick, with a tiny head
of red fire, wriggled in its pool.
The shadows flickered: the Heart beat!

Minstrel

He trailed a zither from
melancholy pale fingers, sighing.
A mist of tears lay still upon the land.

The fire burned down in the grate.
A light burned on the bare ceiling.
A dry teacup stained the oil cloth
where I wrote, bent like a feeding thing
over my own source.

175

A spoonful of white ash fell
with a soundless puff, undetected.
A shadow, or the chill of night,
advanced out of the corner.
I stopped, my hand lifted
an inch from the page.

Outside, the heavens listened,
a starless diaphragm
stopped miles overhead
to hear the remotest whisper
of returning matter, missing
an enormous black beat.

The earth stretched out in answer.
Little directionless instincts
uncoiled from the wet mud-cracks,
crept in wisps of purpose, and vanished
leaving momentary traces
of claw marks, breasts,
ribs, feathery prints,

eyes shutting and opening
all over the surface.
A distant point of light
winked at the edge of nothing.

A knock on the window
and everything in fantasy fright
flurried and disappeared.
My father looked in from the dark,
my face black-mirrored beside his.

His Father's Hands

I drank firmly
and set the glass down between us firmly.
You were saying.

My father.
Was saying.

His finger prodded and prodded,
marring his point. Emphas-
emphasemphasis.

I have watched
his father's hands before him

     cupped, and tightening the black Plug
between knife and thumb,
carving off little curlicues
to rub them in the dark of his palms,

or cutting into new leather at his bench,
levering a groove open with his thumb,
insinuating wet sprigs for the hammer.

He kept the sprigs in mouthfuls
and brought them out in silvery
units between his lips.

I took a pinch out of their hole
and knocked them one by one into the wood,
bright points among hundreds gone black,
other children's—cousins and others, grown up.

     Or his bow hand scarcely moving,
scraping in the dark corner near the fire,
his plump fingers shifting on the strings.

To his deaf, inclined head
he hugged the fiddle's body,
whispering with the tune

with breaking heart
whene'er I hear
in privacy, across a blocked void,

the wind that shakes the barley.
The wind . . .
round her grave . . .

on my breast in blood she died . . .
But blood for blood without remorse
I've ta'en . . .

Beyond that.

*

Your family, Thomas, met with and helped
many of the Croppies in hiding from the Yeos
or on their way home after the defeat
in south Wexford. They sheltered the Laceys
who were later hanged on the Bridge in Ballinglen
between Tinahely and Anacorra.

From hearsay, as far as I can tell
the Men Folk were either Stone Cutters
or masons or probably both.
                              In the 18
and late 1700s even the farmers
had some other trade to make a living.

They lived in Farnese among a Colony
of North of Ireland or Scotch settlers left there
in some of the dispersals or migrations
which occurred in this Area of Wicklow and Wexford
and Carlow. And some years before that time
the Family came from somewhere around Tullow.

Beyond that

*

Littered uplands. Dense grass. Rocks everywhere,
wet underneath, retaining memory of the long cold.

First, a prow of land
chosen, and webbed with tracks;
then boulders chosen
and sloped together, stabilized in menace.

I do not like this place.
I do not think the people who lived here
were ever happy. It feels evil.
Terrible things happened.
I feel afraid here when I am on my own.

*

Dispersals or migrations.
Through what evolutions or accidents
toward that peace and patience
by the fireside, that blocked gentleness . . .

That serene pause, with the slashing knife,
in kindly mockery,
as I busy myself with my little nails
at the rude block, his bench.

The blood advancing
—gorging vessel after vessel—
and altering in them
one by one.

Behold, that gentleness already
modulated twice, in others:
to earnestness and iteration;
to an offhandedness, repressing various impulses.

*

Extraordinary . . . The big block—I found it
years afterward in a corner of the yard
in sunlight after rain
and stood it up, wet and black:
it turned under my hands, an axis
of light flashing down its length,
and the wood's soft flesh broke open,
countless little nails
squirming and dropping out of it.

Epilogue

The great cell of nightmare rose in pallor
and shed its glare down on the calm gulf.
A woman waited at the edge, with lank hair.
She spread it out. It stiffened and moved
by itself, glistening on her shoulders.

We squirmed in expectation. Then there rose
a suffused heart, stopped, clenched on its light.
'Reap us!' we hissed, in praise. The heart beat
and broke open, and sent a fierce beam
among our wriggling sheaves.

Caught in her cold fist, I writhed and reversed.

*

Mostly the thing runs smoothly, the fall is cradled
immediately in a motherly warmth, with nothing
to disturb the dark urge, except from within
—a tenseness, as it coils on itself, changing
to obscure substance.

Anxieties pass through it,
but it can make no sense of them. It knows
only that it is nightmare-bearing tissue
and that there are others. They drift together
through 'incommunicable' dark, one by one,

toward the dawn zone, not knowing or caring
that they share anything.
                    Awakening,
their ghost-companionship dissolves back
into private shadow, not often called upon.

A TECHNICAL SUPPLEMENT (1976)

My dear master, I am over forty. I am tired out with tricks and shufflings. I cry from morning till night for rest, rest; and scarcely a day passes when I am not tempted to go and live in obscurity and die in peace in the depths of my old country. There comes a time when all ashes are mingled. Then what will it boot me to have been Voltaire or Diderot, or whether it is your three syllables or my three syllables that survive? One must work, one must be useful, one owes an account of one's gifts, etcetera, etcetera. Be useful to men! Is it quite clear that one does more than amuse them, and that there is much difference between the philosopher and the flute-player? They listen to one and the other with pleasure or disdain, and remain what they were. The Athenians were never wickeder than in the time of Socrates, and perhaps all they owe to his existence is a crime the more. That there is more spleen than good sense in all this, I admit—and back to the Encyclopaedia I go.

—Diderot to Voltaire, 19 February 1758, *trans.* John Viscount Morley

Prologue

No one did anything at first.
There was no hope.
We were slumped there in the dark, like lead.
Anyone could have done anything with us.

Then someone with backbone made a move
—wherever he found the energy—
and started wriggling away.

After a while another set out across the mud
calling back uneasily for anybody else.
The voice, in a momentary stillness, echoed.
We heard sharp breathing, and then
a body floundering off in the wet.

Then a third.
That decided it for me.
I felt the whole past and future pressing on me,
the millions—even the One!—
that might not live unless . . .
I swore there would be no waste. No waste!

I started. There was one more after me
then the whole world exploded behind us
and a golden light blasted us out.

We found each other afterwards,
inert and stunned, but alive.
Five.

1

Blessed William Skullbullet
glaring from the furnace of your hair
thou whose definitions—whose insane nets—
plunge and convulse to hold thy furious catch
let our gaze blaze, we pray,
let us see how the whole thing

works

2

You will note firstly that there is no containing skin
as we understand it, but 'contained' muscles
—separate entities, interwound and overlaid,
firm, as if made of fish-meat or some
stretched blend of fibre and fat.
This one, for example, containing—functioning *as*—
a shoulderblade; or this one like a strap
reaching underneath it, its tail
melting into a lower rib; or this one
nuzzling into the crease of the groin;
or this, on the upper arm, like a big leech;
even the eyes—dry staring buttons of muscle.
It would seem possible to peel the body asunder,
to pick off the muscles and let them
drop away one by one writhing
until you had laid bare
four or five simple bones at most.
Except that at the first violation
the body would rip into pieces and fly apart
with terrible spasms.

3

A figure struck and lodged in the earth
    and squatted, buried to the knees.
It stared, absolutely tense.
    Time passed.

It settled gradually
    working like a root into the soil.
After it was fixed firmly
    the pent energy released inward.

Clarity and lightness
    opened in the hollow of the head.
Articulation, *capacity*,
    itched in the thumbs and fingers.

The heart fibres loosened as they dried
    and tangled back among themselves.
The whole interior of the body
    became an empty dry space.

The stare faded in the eyes
    which grew watchful, then passive
—lenses, letting the light pass easily
    in either direction.

The face went solid
    and set in a thick mask
on jaws and neck.
    The lips adhered.

The brow went blank.
    Hands and fingers found each other
and joined on his lap.
    He grew weightless,

the solid posture
    grew graceful.
A light architecture.
    No-stress against no-stress.

The seam of the lips
  widened minutely in a smile.
The outer corners of the eyes crinkled.
  The lenses grew opaque, and began to glow.

And so he departed, leaving a mere shell
  —that serene effigy
we have copied so much
  and set everywhere:

on mountaintops, at the sources of streams,
  hid in caves, sunk in the depths of the sea,
perched on pillars in the desert,
  fixed in tree forks,

on car bonnets, on the prows
  of ships and trains,
stood on shelves, in fanlights,
  over stable doors, planted under foundation stones,

attached to our women
  in miniature: on their ears
or at their wrists, or disappearing on pendants
  down their dark bosoms.

4

The point, greatly enlarged
pushed against the skin
depressing an area of tissue.
Rupture occurred: at first a separation
at the intensest place among the cells
then a deepening damage
with nerve-strings fraying
and snapping and writhing back.
Blood welled up to fill the wound,
bathing the point as it went deeper.

Persist.
          Beyond a certain depth
it stands upright by itself
and quivers with borrowed life.

Persist.
          And you may find
the buried well. And take on
the stillness of a root.

Quietus.

          Or:

5

A blade licks out and acts
with one tongue.
Jets of blood respond
in diverse tongues.

And promptly.
A single sufficient cut
and the body drops at once.
No reserve. Inert.

If you would care to enter this grove of beasts:

6

A veteran smiled and let us pass through
to the dripping groves in Swift's slaughterhouse,
hot confusion and the scream-rasp of the saw.
Huge horned fruit not quite dead
—chained, hooked by one hock, stunned
above a pool of steaming spiceblood.

Two elderly men in aprons waded back and forth
with long knives they sharpened slowly and
inserted, tapping cascades of black blood
that collapsed before their faces onto the concrete.
Another fallen beast landed, kicking,
and was hooked by the ankle and hoisted into its place.

They come in behind a plank barrier on an upper level
walking with erect tail to the stunning place . . .
Later in the process they encounter
a man who loosens the skin around their tails
with deep cuts in unexpected directions;
the tail springs back; the hide pulls down to the jaws.

With the sheep it was even clearer
they were dangling alive, the blood trickling
over nostrils and teeth. A flock of them waited their turn
crowded into the furthest corner of the pen,
some looking back over their shoulders
at us, in our window.

Great bulks of pigs hung from dainty heels,
the full sow-throats cut open the wrong way.
Three negroes stood on a raised bench before them.
One knifed the belly open upward to the tail
until the knife and his hands disappeared
in the fleshy vulva and broke some bone.

The next opened it downward to the throat,
embraced the mass of entrails, lifted them out
and dropped them in a chute. And so to one
who excavated the skull through flaps of the face,
hooked it onto the carcass and pushed all forward
toward a frame of blue flames, the singeing machine.

At a certain point it is all merely meat,
sections hung or stacked in a certain order.
Downstairs a row of steel barrows
holds the liquid heaps of organs.
As each new piece drops, adding itself,
the contents tremble throughout their mass.

In a clean room a white-coated worker
positioned a ham, found a blood vessel with a forceps,
clipped it to a tube of red chemical
and pumped the piece full. It swelled immediately
and saturated: tiny crimson jets
poured from it everywhere. Transfused!

7

Vital spatterings. Excess.
Make the mind creep. Play-blood
bursting everywhere out of
big chopped dolls: the stuff breaking copiously
out of a slow, horrified head.

Is it all right to do this?
Is it an offence against justice
when someone stumbles away helplessly
and has to sit down
until her sobbing stops?

8

How to put it . . . without offence
—even though it is an offence,
monstrous, in itself.

A living thing swallowing another.

Lizards:
          Stone still
holding it sideways in its jaws.
With a jerk, adjusting it
with the head facing nearer.

189

The two staring in separate directions.

Again. The head inside the mouth
and the little hands and feet and the tail
and the suddenly soft round belly
hanging down outside.

                    Again.
Splayed hind legs and a tail.

A tail.
        Then
a leather-granite face
unfulfillable.

9

A dark hall. Great green liquid windows
lit. The Stations of the Depths.

In its deep tank, a leopard shark patrolled
away from the window, enlarging to a shadow.
It circled back, grew brighter, reduced
into blunt focus—a pink down-laugh, white needles—
and darkened away again, lengthening.

A herring-flock pelted in spinning water
staring in place—they trembled with speed
and fled, shifted and corrected,
strung together invisibly in their cluster.

Two morays craned up their exposed shoulders
from a cleft, the bird-beaked heads
peering up at a far off music of slaughter,
moving with it, thick and stiff.

A still tank. Gross anemones flowered open
flesh-brilliant on slopes of rock.
A crayfish, crusted with black detail, dreamed
on twig tips across the bottom sand.
A crab fumbled at the lip of a coral shelf
and a gentle fish cruised outward, and down.

10

It is so peaceful at last:
sinking onward into a free reverie
—if you weren't continually nudged awake
by little scratching sounds
and brushing sounds outside the door
or muffled voices upstairs.

The idea was to be able to step out
into a clean brightness onto a landing
flooded with sun and blowing gauze
like a cool drunkenness, with every speck of dust
filtered out of the air!
To follow the graceful curve of handrail
and relish the new firmness underfoot,
the very joists giving off confidence.

What an expanse of neglect
stretched before us!
Strip to the singlet and prepare,
fix the work with a steady eye,
begin: scraping and scraping
down to the wood,
making it good, treating it.
Growing unmethodical after a while,
letting the thing stain and stay unfinished.

And we are going to have to do something
about the garden. All that sour soil
stuffed with mongrel growth
—hinges and bits of slate,
gaspipes plugged with dirt.
Disturb anything and there is
a scurrying of wireworms and ribbed woodlice
or a big worm palely deciding.

That door banging again.
If there is anything I can't stand . . .

We have to dig down,
sieve, scour and roughen;
make it all fertile and vigorous
—get the fresh rain down!

11

The shower is over.
And there's the sun out again
and the sound of water outside
trickling clean into the shore.
And the little washed bird-chirps and trills.

A watered peace. Drop. At the heart.
Drop. The unlikely heart.

A shadow an instant
on the window. A bird.
And the sun is gone in again.

(Good withdrawn, that other good may come.)

We have shaped and polished.
We have put a little darkness behind us,
we are out of that soup.
Into a little brightness.
That soup.

The mind flexes.
The heart encloses.

12

It might be just as well not to worry too much
about our other friend.

He was mainly captious and fanciful.
Gifted, certainly, but finally he leaves
a shrug of disappointment.
Good company from time to time
but it was best kept offhand.
Any regularity, any intimacy,
and the veneer . . . Mean as a cat,
always edging for the small advantage.

But he *could* compete.
There isn't a day passes but I thank God
some others I know—I can see them, mounting up
with grim pleasure to the judgement seat—
didn't 'fulfil their promise'.

An arrogant beginning, *then*
the hard attrition.
              Stomach that
and you find a kind of strength not to be had
any other way. Enforced humility,
with all the faculties. Making for
a small excellence—very valuable.

There, at the unrewarding outer reaches,
the integrity of the whole thing is tested.

13

Hand lifted. Song.
                    I hear.
Hand on breast. Dear heart.
                              I know.
Hand at the throat. Funnelled blood.
                                    It is yours.
Hand over eyes. I see.
                    I see.

14

My eye hurt. I lay down
and pressed it shut into
the palm of my hand.

I slept uneasily
        a dish of ripe eyes gaped up
        at the groaning iron press descending
                    and dreamed
I pulled a sheet of brilliant colour
free from the dark.

15

The pen writhed. It moved
under my thumb!
                    It has sensed
that sad prowler on our landing again.

If she dares come nearer, if she dares . . .
She and her 'sudden and
peremptory incursions' . . .
I'll pierce her like
a soft fruit, a soft big seed!

16

The penetrating senses, the intimacy,
the detailed warmth, the touch under the shirt,
all these things, they cling, they delight,
they hold us back. It is a question of
getting separated from one's habits
and stumbling onto another way. The beginning
must be inward. Turn inward. Divide.

A few times in a lifetime, with luck,
the actual *substance* alters: fills with
expectation, beats with a molten glow
as change occurs; grows cool; resumes.

There is a pause at the full
without currents or wind. The shorescape
holds its thousand mirrors and waits.
Weed rustles in a cleft
and it is not the wind. In a nearby pool
elements of memory are stalking one another.

17

A smell of hot home-made loaves
came from the kitchen downstairs.

A sheet of yellowish Victorian thick paper,
a few spearheads depicted in crusty brown ink
—Viking remains at Islandbridge—
added their shiny-stale smell to the baked air
like dried meat.

              Man-meat, spitted.
Corpses scattered on the river mud
in suds of blood, a few here and there
with broken-off spears buried in them,
buried with them, preserving the points
unweathered for a period.

> For, let me see . . .

a few years—say a lifetime—
(That bread smells delicious!)
over the even thousand years.

18

Asia: great deserts of grass
with poppies and distant cities trembling
in the golden wind. Whole centuries
(if I have it even partly right)
valuing passive watchfulness—not to fuss.

Ah well.

> Grind it up, wash it down,

stoke the blind muscular furnace,
keep the waste volatile
—sieve it: scoop and shake, shiver and tilt.

Reach up expertly in your shiny boots,
tinker and trim, empty your oil-can
into the hissing navels, tap the flickering dials,
study the massive shimmering accurate flywheels.

It isn't the kind of job you can do properly
without a proper lunch: fresh bread,
ham, a piece of cheese,
an apple, a flask of coffee.

> Enjoy it

on your deafening bench.

> Outlandish

the things that will come into your mind.
Often you will find yourself standing up
snapping your fingers suddenly
and there's a thing for you!
And you give a skip up the shop-floor.

19

It is hard to beat a good meal
and a turn on the terrace,
or a picnic on the beach at evening,
watching the breakers blur and gleam
as the brain skews softly.
Or an enjoyable rest, with a whodunit
under a flowering chestnut, an essay or two
on a park bench, a romance devoured
at one stroke on a grassy slope.

But for real pleasure there is nothing to equal
sitting down to a *serious* read,
getting settled down comfortably for the night
with a demanding book on your knee
and your head intent over it,
eyes bridging the gap, closing a circuit.

Except that it is not a closed circuit,
more a mingling of lives, worlds simmering
in the entranced interval: all that you are
and have come to be
—or as much as can be brought to bear—
'putting on' the fixed outcome of another's
encounter with what what he was
and had come to be
impelled him to stop in flux, living,
and hold that encounter out from
the streaming away of lifeblood, timeblood,
a nexus a nexus
wriggling with life not of our kind.

Until one day as I was . . .

I met a fair maid all shining
with hair all over her cheeks
and pearly tongue
who spoke to me and sighed
as if my own nervous nakedness
spoke to me and said:

My heart is a black fruit.
It is a piece of black coal.
When I laugh a black thing hovers.

20

Loneliness. An odour of soap.
To this end must we come,
deafened with spent energy.

And so the years propel themselves onward
toward that tunnel, and the stink of fear.

—We can amend that. (Time permits
a certain latitude. Not much,
but a harmless re-beginning.)

'And so the years propel themselves
onward on thickening scars, toward
new efforts of propulsion . . .'

21

The residue of a person's work.

The words 'water' or 'root'
offered in real refreshment. The words
'Love', 'Truth', etc., offered with force
but self-serving, therefore ineffective.
A fading pose—the lonely prowl of the outcast.

Or half a dozen outward howls of glory
and noble despair. Borrowed glory,
his own despair. For the rest, energy wasted
grimacing facetiously inward. And yet
a vivid and lasting image: the racked outcast.

Or opinion modified or sharpened, in search.
Emotion expelled, to free the structure of a thing,
or indulged, to free the structure of an idea.
The entirety of one's being
crowded for everlasting shelter
into the memory of one crust of bread.
Granting it everlasting life.
Eating it absolutely.

Somehow it all matters ever after—very much—
though each little thing matters little
however painful that may be.

And remember that foolishness
though it may give access to heights of vision
in certain gifted abnormal brains
remains always what it is.

22
Where is everybody?
                    Look
in the mirror, at that face.

It began to separate, the head opening
like a rubbery fan.
The thin hair blurred and crept apart
widening from a deepening seam
as the forehead opened down the centre
and unfolded pale new detail
surfacing from within.

The eyes moved wider apart
and another eye surfaced between them and divided.
The nose divided and doubled and moved out
one to right and left.
The mouth stretched in a snarl
then split into two mouths, pursed.

Two faces now returned my stare
each whole yet neither quite 'itself'.
(But then the original could not
have been called 'itself' either.
What but some uneasiness made it divide?)

At any rate my stare now began
to grow unfixed, wandering
from one image to the other
as if losing conviction.

Another ounce of impulse and
I might have driven my fist at the mirror
and abolished everything.
But the starred ruins
would only have started to divide and creep.

23

That day when I woke
a great private blade
was planted in me from bowels to brain.
I lay there alive round it. When I moved
it moved with me, and there was no hurt.
I knew it was not going to go away.
I got up carefully, transfixed.

From that day forth I knew
what it was to taste reality
and not to; to suffer tedium or pain
and not to; to eat, swallowing with pleasure,
and not to; to yield and fail,
to note this or that withering in me,
and not to; to anticipate
the Breath, the Bite, with cowering arms.

(Tiny delicate dawn-antelope that go without water
getting all they need in vegetation and the dew.
Night-staring jerboa.
The snapping of their slender bones,
rosy flesh bursting in small sweet screams
against the palate fine. Just a quick
note. Lest we forget.)

Meanwhile, with enormous care,
to the split id—delicate
as a flintflake—the knifed nous.

24

It is time I continued my fall.

The divider waits, shaped
razor sharp to my dream print.

I should feel nothing.

Turning slowly and more slowly
we drifted to rest in a warmth of flesh,
twinned, glaring and growing.

He carried me out of the lamplight.
I hugged his night-smelling overcoat
and let myself loosen with his steps
and my sight swim.
                              Sticks in a black hedge
went flickering past. Frosty twinkles
danced along in the granite.

The light on the next lamp-post
stepped nearer, blue-white, gas-cold.
Nearer, and the living mantle
licked and hummed in its heart.
A stern moon-stare shed all over my brain
as he carried me, warm and chill,
homeward, abandoned, onward to the next shadow.

C. G. Jung's 'First Years'

1

Dark waters churn amongst us
and whiten against troublesome obstacles:

A nurse's intimate warm ear
far in the past; the sallow loin of her throat;
and more—her song at twilight
as she dreamily (let us now suppose)
combined in her entrails
memories of womanly manipulations
with further detailed plans for the living flesh.

203

2

Jesus, and his graves eating the dead.
A Jesuit—a witchbat—
toiled with outspread sleeves down
the path from a wooded hilltop.
A pillar of skin
stared up dumb, enthroned
in an underground room.

The dreams broke in succession and ran back
whispering with disappearing particulars.

*

Since when I have eaten Jesus.
And stepped onto the path
  long ago: my fingers stretched at the hill
  and a sleeve-winged terror
  shrank like a shadow and flapped away
  sailing over the dry grass;
  staring crumbs led up through the tree-darkness
  to a hollow, with bloody steps down.
And have assumed the throne.

Anniversaries

1955

He took her, trembling
with decision, into a cage
of flowering arches full of light
to the altar.

They squeezed hands
and waited in happiness.
They were creatures to catch
Nature's attention.

(The three qualities that are necessary
She has, namely: patience,
deliberation,
and skill with the instruments.)

*

And very soon
we were moving outward
together, a fraction
apart.

We preened and shivered
among pale stems
under nodding grain. Breezes nibbled
and fingered at our fur.

We advanced with care.
Sunlight passed direct
into our blood.
Mercury

       glittered
in the needle-nails we
sank into the tissuey stems
as we climbed

eyeing each other,
on whom
Nature had as yet
worked so little.

1956

Fifteen minutes or thereabouts
of Prelude and Liebestod
—elephant into orgasm—
and I was about ready.

I crooked my foot
around the chair-leg
and my fingers around
the pen, and set

the star-dome
creaking with music
at absolute zero
across the bankrupt night.

A couple of hundred yards around the corner
in a moon-flooded office in Merrion Street
my Finance files dreamed,
propped at the ledge,

my desk moved
                    infinitesimally.
Over the entire country,
over market and harbour, in silvery light,

emanations of government
materialised and embraced
downward and began
metaphysically to bite.

A small herd of friends
stared back from the Mailboat rail.
A mongrel dog lapped
in a deserted town square.

A book came
fluttering out of the dark
and flapped
at the window.

1975

'Below us in the distance
we came upon
a wide wheatfield breathing
dust-gold.

We flew down
and our claws curled, as one,
around the same outer branch
steadily, as it shook.

Our eyes thrilled
together: loaded
stems dipped everywhere
under mouse-fruit.'

1975
an alternative

'Once in the long flight we swerved low,
supported on each other's presences.
Our shadows raced flickering over stubble
sprinkled with eyepoints of fierce fright and malice.

The urge to strangle at them with our feet!

Then re-ascended.'

> *A species of wide range,*
they feed generally at height,
the more enduring as they grow tireder;
starving if needs be; living on their own waste.

Artists' Letters

Folders, papers, proofs, maps
with tissue paper marked and coloured.
I was looking for something,
confirmation of something,
in the cardboard box
when my fingers deflected among
fat packets of love letters,
old immediacies in elastic bands.

I shook a letter open from
its creases, carefully, and read
—and shrugged, embarrassed.
                              Then stirred.
My hand grew thin and agitated
as the words crawled again
quickly over the dried paper.

Letter by letter the foolishness
deepened, but displayed
a courage in its own unsureness;
acknowledged futility and waste
in all their importance . . . a young idiocy
in desperate full-hearted abandon
to all the chance of one choice:

There is one throw, no more. One
offering: make it. With no style
—these are desperate times. There is
a poverty of spirit in the wind;
a shabby richness in braving it.
My apologies, but you are my beloved
and I will not be put off.

What is it about such letters,
torn free ignominiously
in love? Character stripped off
our pens plunge repeatedly
at the unique cliché, cover
ache after ache of radiant paper
with analytic ecstasies,
wrestle in repetitious fury.

The flesh storms our brain; we storm
our entranced opposite, badger her
with body metaphors, project
our selves with out-thrust stuttering arms,
cajoling, forcing her
—her spread-eagled spirit—
to accept our suspect cries
with shocked and shining eyes.

Artists' letters (as the young career
grows firmer in excited pride
and moves toward authority
after the first facetiousness,
the spirit shaken into strength
by shock after shock of understanding)
suddenly shudder and *display*! Animal.
Violent vital organs of desire.

A toothless mouth opens
and we throw ourselves, enthralled, against our bonds
and thrash toward her. And when we have
been nicely eaten and our parts
spat out whole and have become
'one', *then* we can settle our cuffs
and our Germanic collar
and turn back calmly toward distinguished things.

Tao and Unfitness at Inistiogue on the River Nore

Noon

The black flies kept nagging in the heat.
Swarms of them, at every step, snarled
off pats of cow dung spattered in the grass.

Move, if you move, like water.

The punts were knocking by the boathouse, at full tide.
Volumes of water turned the river curve
hushed under an insect haze.

                         Slips of white,
trout bellies, flicked in the corner of the eye
and dropped back onto the deep mirror.

Respond. Do not interfere. Echo.

Thick green woods along the opposite bank
climbed up from a root-dark recess
eaved with mud-whitened leaves.

*

In a matter of hours all that water is gone,
except for a channel near the far side.
Muck and shingle and pools where the children
wade, stabbing flatfish.

Afternoon

Inistiogue itself is perfectly lovely,
like a typical English village, but a bit sullen.
Our voices echoed in sunny corners
among the old houses; we admired
the stonework and gateways, the interplay
of roofs and angled streets.

The square, with its 'village green', lay empty.
The little shops had hardly anything.
The Protestant church was guarded by a woman
of about forty, a retainer, spastic
and indistinct, who drove us out.

An obelisk to the Brownsfoords and a Victorian
Celto-Gothic drinking fountain, erected
by a Tighe widow for the villagers,
'erected' in the centre. An astronomical-looking
sundial stood sentry on a platform
on the corner where High Street went up out of the square.

We drove up, past a long-handled water pump
placed at the turn, with an eye to the effect,
then out of the town for a quarter of a mile
above the valley, and came to the dead gate
of Woodstock, once home of the Tighes.

*

The great ruin presented its flat front
at us, sunstruck. The children disappeared.
Eleanor picked her way around a big fallen branch
and away along the face toward the outbuildings.
I took the grassy front steps and was gathered up
in a brick-red stillness. A rook clattered out of the dining room.

A sapling, hooked thirty feet up
in a cracked corner, held out a ghost-green
cirrus of leaves. Cavities
of collapsed fireplaces connected silently
about the walls. Deserted spaces, complicated
by door-openings everywhere.

There was a path up among bushes and nettles
over the beaten debris, then a drop, where bricks
and plaster and rafters had fallen into the kitchens.
A line of small choked arches . . . The pantries, possibly.

Be still, as though pure.

A brick, and its dust, fell.

Nightfall

The trees we drove under in the dusk
as we threaded back along the river through the woods
were no mere dark growth, but a flitting-place
for ragged feeling, old angers and rumours.

Black and Tan ghosts up there, at home
on the Woodstock heights: an iron mouth
scanning the Kilkenny road: the house
gutted by the townspeople and burned to ruins.

The little Ford we met, and inched past, full of men
we had noticed along the river bank during the week,
disappeared behind us into a fifty-year-old night.
Even their caps and raincoats . . .

Sons, or grandsons, Poachers.
                              Mud-tasted salmon
slithering in a plastic bag around the boot,
bloodied muscles, disputed since King John.

The ghosts of daughters of the family
waited in the uncut grass as we drove
down to our mock-Austrian lodge and stopped.

*

We untied the punt in the half-light, and pushed out
to take a last hour on the river, until night.
We drifted, but stayed almost still.
The current underneath us
and the tide coming back to the full
cancelled in a gleaming calm, punctuated
by the plop of fish.

Down on the water . . . at eye level . . . in the little light
remaining overhead . . . the mayfly passed in a loose drift,
thick and frail, a hatch slow with sex,
separate morsels trailing their slack filaments,
olive, pale evening dun, imagoes, unseen eggs
dropping from the air, subimagoes, the river filled
with their nymphs ascending and excited trout.

Be subtle, as though not there.

We were near the island—no more than a dark mass
on a sheet of silver—when a man appeared in mid-river
quickly and with scarcely a sound, his paddle touching
left and right of the prow, with a sack behind him.
The flat cot's long body slid past effortless
as a fish, sinewing from side to side,
as he passed us and vanished.

Song of the Night

Philadelphia

A compound bass roar
an ocean voice
Metropolis in the ear
soft-thundered among the towers below
breaking in a hiss of detail
but without wave-rhythm
without breath-rhythm
exhalation without cease
amplified
of terrible pressure
interrupted by brief blasts and nasal shouts
guttural diesels
a sky-train waning in a line of thunder.

I opened the great atlas on the desk.

The Atlantic curved on the world.

Carraroe

Our far boundary was Gorumna island
low on the water, dotted
with granite erratics, extended grey-green
along the opposite shore of the bay
toward the south Connemara series.

On our shore, among a tumble of boulders
on the minced coral, there was one
balanced with rugged edge upward,
stuck with limpets. Over it,
with the incoming tide, the waters

wash back and forth irregularly
and cover and uncover the brown angles.
Films of liquid light run
shimmering, cut by shell-points, over
stone inclines and clotted buds of anemones.

The films fatten with plasm and flow and fill
more loosely over the rock and gradually drown it.
Then larger movements invade from further out,
from the depths,
alive and in movement. At night-time,

in the wind, at that place,
the water-wash lapped at itself under the rocks
and withdrew rustling down the invisible grains.
The ocean worked in dark masses in the bay
and applied long leverage at the shore.

*

We were finished, and quiet.
The music was over.
The lamp hissed in the tent.

We collected the cooking things
and plates and mugs and cutlery
scattered around us in the grass,
everything bone cold,
and put it all in the basin.

I unhooked the lamp and made my way down
flickering over the rocks with the children
to the edge of the ocean.

A cell of light hollowed around us
out of the night. Splashes and clear voices echoed
as the spoons and knives were dug down
and enamel plates scooped under water
into the sand, and scraped and rinsed.

I held the lamp out a little over the sea.
Silvery sand-eels seethed everywhere we stepped:
shivered and panicked through the shallows,
vanished—became sand—were discovered,
picked up with exclamations,
held out damp and deathly,
little whips fainted away
in wet small palms, in an iodine smell.

*

She was standing in a sheltered angle,
urgent and quiet.
                    'Look back.'

The great theatre of Connemara,
dark. A cloud bank stretched in folds
across the sky, luminous
with inner activity.

Centred on the beached lamp
a single cell of cold light
—part land and part living water—
blazed with child voices.

They splashed about the stark red basin,
pouncing. They lifted it and consulted.
Their crystalline laughter escaped upward,
their shadows huge.

*

We made off toward the rocky point
past the tent's walls flapping.

A new music came on the wind: string sounds hissing
mixed with a soft inner-ear roar
blown off the ocean; a persistent
tympanum double-beat ('. . . darkly expressive,
coming from innermost depths . . .') That old
body music. *Schattenhaft.* SONG OF THE NIGHT.
A long horn call, 'a single note
that lingers, changing colour as it fades . . .'

Overhead a curlew responded.
'poignant . . .' Yes.
'hauntingly beautiful . . .' Yes!

The bay—every inlet—lifted
and glittered toward us in articulated light.
The land, a pitch-black stage
of boulder shapes and scalps of heaped weed,
inhaled.

             A part of the mass
grated and tore, cranking harshly,
and detached and struggled upward
and beat past us along the rocks,
bat-black, heron-slow.

THE MESSENGER (1978)

In memory of John Paul Kinsella
(died May 1976)

For days I have wakened and felt immediately
half sick at something. Hour follows hour
but my shoulders are chilled with expectation.

It is more than mere Loss

                   (your tomb-image
drips and blackens, my leaden root
curled on your lap)

               or 'what you missed'.
(The hand conceives an impossible Possible
and exhausts in mid-reach.
What could be more natural?)

Deeper. A suspicion in the bones
as though they too could melt in filth.

Something to discourage goodness.

A moist movement within.
A worm winds on its hoard.
A dead egg glimmers—a pearl in muck
glimpsed only as the muck settles.

1

His mother's image settled on him
out of the dark, at the last,
and the Self sagged, unmanned.

Corded into a thick dressing gown
he glared from his rocker
at people *whispering* on television.

He knocked the last drops of Baby Power
into his glass and carried the lifewater
to his lips. He recollected himself

and went on with a story out of Guinness's
—the Brewery pension 'abated' by 'an amount
equal to the amount' of some pittance

on some Godforsaken pretext.
His last battle—the impulse
at its tottering extreme:

muster your fellow pensioners, and advance
pitched with them
                    ('Power to the Spent!')

against the far off boardroom door.
All about him, open mouthed,
they expired in ones and twos.

Somebody well dressed
pressed my hand in the graveyard.
A thoughtful delegated word or two:

'His father before him . . . Ah, the barge captain . . .
A valued connection. He will be well remembered . . .
He lived in his two sons.'

In his own half fierce force
he lived! And stuck the first brand shakily
under that good family firm,

formed their first Union, and entered their lists.
Mason and Knight gave ground in twostep,
manager and priest disappeared

and reappeared under each other's hats;
in jigtime, to the ever popular
Faith Of Our Fathers, he was high and dry.

And in time was well remembered.
Thumbs in belt, back and forth
in stiff boots he rocked with the news

in front of the fireplace, in his frieze jacket,
with a couple of bottles of Export in the pockets.
Florid and with scorn he stomached it

in full vigour, in his fiftieth year,
every ounce of youth
absorbed into his body.

For there is really nothing to be done.
There is an urge, and it is valuable,
but it is of no avail.

He brandished his solid body
thirty feet high above their heads therefore
and with a shout of laughter

traversed a steel beam in the Racking Shed
and dared with outstretched arms
what might befall.

And it befell that summer,
after the experimental doses,
that his bronchi wrecked him with coughs

and the muffled inner
heartstopping little
hammerblows began.

*

A brave leap
in full heart
into full stop.

On bright prospects
sable: a slammed
door.

Vaunt and check.
Cursus inter-
ruptus.

Typically, there is a turning away.
The Self is islanded in fog.
It is meagre and plagued with wants

but secure. Every positive matter
that might endanger—but also enrich—
is banished. The banished matter

(a cyst, in effect, of the subject's aspirations
painful with his many disappointments)
absorbs into the psyche, where it sleeps.

Intermittently, when disturbed, it wakes
as a guardian—or 'patron'—monster
with characteristic conflicting emotional claims:

appalling, appealing; exacting sympathy
even as it threatens. (Our verb 'to haunt'
preserves the ambiguity exactly.)

A dragon slashes its lizard wings
as it looks out, with halved head,
and bellows with incompleteness.

*

Often, much too familiar for comfort,
the beast was suddenly there
insinuating between us:

'Who'd like to know what *I* know?'
'Who has a skeleton in *his* meat cupboard?'

'Who is inclined to lapse and let
the bone go with the dog?'

'Who flings off in a huff
and never counts the cost
as long as there's a bitter phrase
to roll around on the tongue?'

'When Guess Who polished his pointy shoe
and brushed his brilliantine
to whose admiring gaze
guess who hoodwinked Who?'

Or it would sigh and say:
'Guess who'd love to gobble *you* up?'
Or 'Who'd like to see what *I* have?'

*

I would. And have followed
the pewtery heave of hindquarters
into the fog, the wings down at heel,

until back there in the dark
the whole thing
fell on its face.

And blackened . . . And began
melting its details and dripping them away
little by little to reveal

him (supine, jutjawed and
incommunicable, privately
surrendering his tissues and traps).

And have watched my hand reach in under
after something, and felt it
close upon it and ease him of it.

The eggseed Goodness
that is also called
Decency.

2

Goodness is where you find it.
Abnormal.
        A pearl.

A milkblue
blind orb.
        Look in it:

It is outside the Black Lion, in Inchicore.
A young man. He is not much more than thirty.
He is on an election lorry, trying to shout.

He is goodlooking and dark.
He has a raincoat belted tight
and his hair is brushed back, like what actor.

He is shouting about the Blueshirts
but his voice is hoarse.
His arm keeps pointing upward.

I am there. A dark little
blackvelvet-eyed jew-child
with leaflets.

A big Dublin face
leans down with a moustache, growling
it is a scandal.

*

The Oblate Fathers was packed.
I sat squeezed against a cold pillar.
A bull-voice rang among the arches.

I made faces at my ghost in the brawn marble.
The round shaft went up shining
into a mouth of stone flowers

and the angry words echoed
among the hanging lamps,
off the dark golden walls.

He covered my hand with his
and we started getting out
in the middle of Mass past everybody.

Father Collier's top half in the pulpit
in a muscular black soutane and white lace
grabbed the crimson velvet ledge

—thick white hair, a red face,
a black mouth shouting
Godless Russia after us.

*

It is an August evening, in Wicklow.
It is getting late. They have tussled in love.
They are hidden, near the river bank.

They lie face up in the grass, not touching,
head close to head, a woman and her secret husband.
A gossamer ghost arrows and hesitates

out of the reeds, and stands in the air above them
insect-shimmering, and settles on a bright
inner upturn of her dress. The wings

close up like palms. The body, a glass worm,
is pulsing. The tail-tip winces and quivers:

I *think* there is where I come in.

It is! It is! Hurry!
says the great womb-whisper.
Quick! I am all egg!

*

Inside, it is bare but dimly alive.
Such light as there is comes in overcast
through a grey lace curtain across the window,

diffuses in the dust above the bench
and shows him stooped over his last
in a cobbler's shop. He is almost still a boy:

his hands are awkwardly readying something,
his face and shoulders are soft-handsome,
pale silver, ill at ease in the odour-bearing light.

The rest is obscure, swallowed back
in man-smells of leather and oily metal
and the faintest musk.

Beside him, his father's leaden skull
is inclined, gentle and deaf,
above the work on his apron.

The old lion-shoulders expand in the Guinness jersey,
the jaws work in his cheeks
as the quivering awl

pierces the last hole in a sole with a grunt.
He wheezes and pulls it out, and straightens.
The tide is rising and the river runs fast

into the middle span of the last bridge.
He touches the funnel on a nerve at the base
and doffs it on its hinge at the last instant

—the smoke occluding—and hauls it up again
gleaming and pluming in open water.
Here and there along the Liffey wall

he is acclaimed in friendly mockery,
humbly, saturninely, returned.
He reaches for needle and thread

patiently, as his son
struggles at the blank iron foot
in his father's den.

He will not stick at this . . . The knife-blades,
the hammers and pincers, the rasps and punches,
the sprigs in their wooden pits,

catching the light on the plank bench
among uppers and tongues and leather scraps
and black stumps of heelball.

He reaches for a hammer,
his jaw jutting as best it can
with Marx, Engels, Larkin

howling with upstretched arms into the teeth
of Martin Murphy and the Church
and a flourish of police batons,

Connolly strapped in a chair
regarding the guns
that shall pronounce his name for ever.

Baton struck,
            gun spat,
and Martin Murphy shall change his hat.

Son and father, upright, right arms raised.
Stretching a thread.
Trying to strike right.

*

Deeper. The room where they all lived
behind the shop. It is dark here too—shut off
by the narrow yard. But it doesn't matter:

it is bustling with pleasure.
A new messenger boy
stands there in uniform, with shining belt!

He is all excitement: arms akimbo,
a thumb crooked by the telegram pouch,
shoes polished, and a way to make in the world.

His eyes are bright,
his schoolmaster's tags fresh in mind.
He has a few of the Gentlemen's Sixpenny Library

under the bed—*A Midsummer Night's Dream*,
Sartor Resartus, *The Divine Comedy*, with a notebook,
Moore's *Melodies*, a trifle shaken . . . Shelley, unbound . . .

He unprops the great Post Office bicycle
from the sewing machine and wheels it through the passage
by odours of apron and cabbage-water and whitewashed damp

through the shop and into the street.
It faces uphill. The urchin mounts. I see
a flash of pedals. And a clean pair of heels!

3

An eye, pale with strain, forms in the dark.
About it the iridescent
untouchable secretions collect.

It is a miracle:
the oddity nestles in slime
functionless, in all its rarity,

purifying nothing.
But nothing can befoul it,
which ought probably to console.

He rolled on rubber tyres
out of the chapel door. The oak box
paused gleaming in the May morning air

and turned, sensing its direction.
Our scattered tribe began gathering itself
and trudged off onto a gravel path after it.

By their own lightness
four girls and three boys separated themselves
out in a ragged band from our dull custom

and moved up close after it, in front,
all shapes and sizes,
grandchildren, colourful and silent.

Settings

Model School, Inchicore

Miss Carney handed us out blank paper and marla,
old plasticine with the colours
all rolled together into brown.

You started with a ball of it
and rolled it into a snake curling
around your hand, and kept rolling it
in one place until it wore down into two
with a stain on the paper.

We always tittered at each other
when we said the adding-up table in Irish
and came to her name.

*

In the second school we had Mr Browne.
He had white teeth in his brown man's face.

He stood in front of the black board
and chalked a white dot.

> 'We are going to start
> decimals.'

> I am going to know
> everything.

*

229

One day he said:
'Out into the sun!'
We settled his chair under a tree
and sat ourselves down delighted
in two rows in the greeny gold shade.

A fat bee floated around
shining amongst us
and the flickering sun
warmed our folded coats
and he said: 'History . . . !'

*

When the Autumn came
and the big chestnut leaves
fell all over the playground
we piled them in heaps
between the wall and the tree trunks
and the boys ran races
jumping over the heaps
and tumbled into them shouting.

*

I sat by myself in the shed
and watched the draught
blowing the papers
around the wheels of the bicycles.

Will God judge
        our most secret thoughts and actions?
God will judge
        our most secret thoughts and actions
and every idle word that man shall speak
he shall render an account of it
on the Day of Judgment.

*

The taste
of ink off
the nib shrank your
mouth.

Phoenix Street

It was dark everywhere.
The two paths were empty.
All in.
All in.

*

I have climbed the narrow turn
of the top stairs, holding
the banisters draped with
trousers and pullovers,
and stood smelling the landing again.

And I have opened the black-stained
double doors of the triangular
press up in the corner,
and his dark nest
stirred with promises:

Ruskin and Engels and Carlyle;
Shakespeare in tiny print,
1927 in dead pencil;

the insurance collection book
in a fat elastic band;
a brown photograph

with four young men
dressed up together
and leaning together in laughter.

Bow Lane

I poked in at the back corner
of the wardrobe, at the blind
standing rolled up. It rustled
like a bat trapped inside.

There was light still coming in
over Corcorans' wall
up to the Blessed Virgin on the shelf
over the grandparents' bed.

They kept Uncle Tom's painting
hanging in there, in a black frame
—a steamer with three funnels,
and TK painted on the foam.

He died in here in 1916
of cancer of the colon. My father heard him
whispering to himself: 'Jesus,
Jesus, let me off.' But nothing worked.

I took the grey animal book
from under the clothes in the drawer
and opened it at the Capuchin monkeys
in their forest home.

I asked Tom Ryan once: 'Tell me the print!'
but he only grinned and said
'I will if you can spell Wednesday.'
With his slithery walk.

They were lighting the lamps
outside in the shop and she started shouting:
'What are you up to in there?
Always stuck in that old room.'

Invocation

Sweet mother, sweet muscle,
predatrix,

always in the midst
yet walking to one side

silent, reticent, rarely seen
yet persistent,

we implore—the subsequent
bustling in the previous:

Judge not.
But judge.

Songs of the Psyche

1

A character, indistinct, entered,
looked about him, and began:

Why had I to wait until I am graceless,
unsightly, and a little nervous of stooping
until I could see

through those clear eyes I had once?
It is time. And I am
shivering as in stupid youth.

Who have stood where I was born
and snapped my bitten fingers!

2

It was time.
                    To settle in
and feel what it is like
to be half safe.

When I think of what I *could* . . .
my brain hammers, and I could
dance!
                    But I settled back and
turned inward.

I smelled at a crack in the dirt
and was taken away
teeth grinding
and eyes alight.

An unholy muttering
lingered on my palms
as I laid them to my cheeks
and slept.

3

(Chew nine times
on the chosen meat
and set it down
outside her door

then when you wake
rat small, rat still,
you will carry her life
in your palms, rat self.)

4

There are certain
ill-chosen spirits

that cower close
on innermost knowledge

and must burrow with special care
to find the shallowest peace.

Their need binds them
and hangs between them.

In special tenderness and mental fire
these wound each other

with every touch
meditative and brutal:

they have eaten
and must eat.

5

What a thing it is
to know a thing
full fifty years

with kindness as of one thing
for another
of only its kind.

A monster bore me
and I bear
a monster with me.

6

I have kissed the inner earth
and the grin of stone upon stone
and it was time again

to surrender
to your
beaten smile

7

And she came by a little-haunted path
with modest run advancing
dancing in her flowers
awkwardly up to me.

It was something
to take a little of the spring
out of a person's step.
She offered me her hands.

I took them in mine
—averse
            but it was enough:
we were no longer two

but a third
            fumbling
ghost at polite ghost
of its own matter.

8

A tree with a twisted trunk;
two trees grown into one.
A heart-carving grown thick,
the cuts so deep.

The leaves reached out past us
and hissed: *We were so fond of you!*
There was a stir of flower heads
about our feet

gold for the first blaze,
red for the rough response,
dark blue for misunderstanding,
jet black for rue,

pale for the
unfinished children
that are
waiting everywhere

9

Night foxes
body masks

tilted up, eyes
a city of lights

a cistern hiss
in their erect ears

they are dreaming
one another

10

The fire was banked,
the kitchen door half open,
the chairs angled where they were left.

A moth fumbled
with its fragile blur
up the tobacco-smelling chimney-corner.

Tireless and lifespans old
the long clock-stick laboured
over the mantelpiece, forth and back.

Behind the kitchen table
with the apron
folded on the butter bowl

they returned into the dark
with murder and girl robbery
in their hearts.

*

A great delicate self
approached her cold face

toward the window,
cheek wide and glowing,

afloat, bright, an O
stopped,

a whole mind
blind overhead.

Pegged to a rafter, bathed in smoke,
splayed in flight,

a great moth of prey,
come from nowhere, stared back.

*

A silk maggot,
a detached hair

bathed in firelight,
I writhed in memory.

11
Come with me
      o'er the crystal stream
where eyelids dart
      in the dappled shallows

to where you wait
        on the farther bank
troubled and pretty
        with tattered basket.

Your feathery flesh
        I will kneel and kiss.
Your slender bones
        I will take in mine.

I will pick a straw
        from your stiffened dress
and so retire
        while the grasses whisper

and leeches wrinkle
        black in the water,
willow leaves
        that have fed on blood.

12

It is time, the night gone,
first light fidgeting under the leaves.
Let us kneel and rinse the crust from the cup.

13

I woke suffocating,
        slipped through a fault
into total dark.

No.

I came to myself
        in the middle of a dark wood,
electric with hope.

Please . . .

Yet it *is* a matter
        of negative release:
of being thrown up

out of a state of storm
        into a state of peace, or sleep,
or a dream, or a system of dreams.

By normal process
        organic darkness would summon
Self firstly into being,

an upright on a flat plain,
        a bone stirs in first clay
and a beam of light

struck and snaked
        glittering across a surface
in multi-meanings and vanishes.

Then stealers of fire;
        dragon slayers; helpful animals;
and ultimately the Cross.

Unless the thing were to be based
        on sexuality
or power.

Notes

A New Beginning

God is good but
He had to start
somewhere out of the ache
of *I am*

and lean Himself
over the mothering pit
in faith
thinking

a mouth
to My kiss
in opening

let there be
remote

Opposites

Love is refreshment
in the recognition of pattern.

Grudging memory is its opposite:
it is revealed in the lips.

Our mouths locked in privacy.
The shadow pattern shifted.

The Little Children

I held her propped
    by the tip of a blunt love finger
against the kitchen wall
    and let her topple forward

one, two, three!
    in laughter and panic
into darkness and fire.

*

Incurious about his own
    breaking and renewing energies,
his developing and abandoned purposes,
    he fixes the pieces in and upon each other

in a series of beginnings
       with feathery touches and brutal fumblings,
in stupefying waste, brooding and light.

*

At the first trace
       of backward pressure
the child grows unusable.

Brotherhood

I stretched out my hand to you.
Brother.

The reason for the impulse was unclear:
your behaviour and your work
are incomprehensible to me.

But I had offered my hand.
We were joined by the soft leather of palms.

The matter resolved itself.
A voice whispered:

It is Spring and no time for kindness;
we must bear in mind the quality of the Fall.

I dropped your hand.

Talent and Friendship

Neither is simple
and neither is handed down.

Either persisted in without change
grows ridiculous

and either at any time
may fail.

If it fail in part
it is made good only in part

and if it come to final failure
accept.

As I remember:
a still youthful witch
moving off sick to death
among the graves and the old men

in sharp argument with her pale son.
He muttering in sharp answer,
deadly familiar,
so unlike.

*

There is no mantle
and it does not descend.

Self-Scrutiny

The threadbare body gathers
with a new consideration
about the hidden bones
that shimmered once like spears
of iris in the mind.
It grows conscious
of its composite parts:

the eyes wet with delicacy
that will yet close
under unopenable marble;

the ear admitting the snarl
of mutabilitie
direct to the brain;

the tongue clung more with understanding
to the roof of the mouth
the more it is loosed in the savour of freedom
or the curse made flesh;

the thumbs and digits
pressed into the temples
at the felt limit of our range.

Self-Release

Possibly you would rather I stopped
—uttering guttural Christ curses
and destroying my nails down the wall
or dashing myself to pieces once and for all
in a fury beside your head?

I will ease it somehow.
I could pull down a clean knife-shaft
two-handed into the brain and worry it
minutely about until there is
glaze and numbness in 'that' area.

Then you would see how charming
it is possible to be,
how fluent and fascinating,
a startlement to all,
internationally, and beyond.

Self-Renewal

Reverently I swung open
the two side mirrors to reveal
everywhere, on a white brow crossed,
two ragged cuts; a wet mouth
held shut; eyes hurt and full.

I peered into these
and their velvet stirred
with the pale secrets of all
the lonely that had ever sat
by their lonely mirrors

studying the shame
that had brought them to sit there
and kiss the icy glass
and recover themselves a little

with icy brow on brow,
and one eye cocked at itself,
until they felt more able
to slip off about their business

with the glass clouding over
a couple of fading eye diagrams.

. . . I remember the elaborate, opulent close of Der Rosenkavalier *filling the mean little space: the unmade single bed, the dusty electric fire glowing in the grate, spattered with butts, Reidy's narrow unfocused face intent in the dark like an animal. I heard Mahler there for the first time . . .*

Overture

For ever and ever
    she wept
for the nth time

overladen with feeling
    and dwelling upon herself
and drawing back

through the luxuriant heavens
    into the light
from whence she came,

the great contralto,
    for her beloved son
pale against the chilly fireplace.

And there goes
    that last lovely heartbeat
of the whole world

like a low terrible string
    plucked
on the great Harp of Life,

a major triad of strings,
    celestes—trombones!—
released from all earthbound tonalities.

*

Will God sit there on the Last Day like that,
        the whole thing played out,
listening to a last echo fade,

staring to one side, just sitting there?
        If only we could wring our talent out,
wring it and wring it dry like that.

A butt flung into a dirty grate.
        Elbows on knees, head bowed
devouring an echo out of nothing.

1

Arms uplifted on the podium,
        the left hand dangling tyrannical;
aetat fünfzig;

the stance flat footed;
        the face a fragile axe,
hard and acid, rapt.

Everything a man can do,
        and more, is done,
the sparse hair thrown back,

the white cuffs flaring,
        the ivory baton flourished
and driven deep.

He sports a little paunch
        but this, in its boxy waistcoat,
merely emphasizes the force of will

we find everywhere
        in his strange work:
the readiness to embrace risk,

tedium, the ignoble,
        to try anything ten times
if so the excessive matter can be settled.

(We have waltzed a while with Disaster,
        coat tails twirling along the precipice,
and She is charmed senseless,

Her harmonies collapse
        at a touch.) Only a double drum
is beating: two hearts coupled.

There is an overpowering tinkle;
        a pregnant hush.
Masterful yet sensitive

his baton explores
        her core of peace,
every rhythm drained

into nothing, the nothingness
        adjusting toward
a new readiness.

From his captive hearers
        (though we can scarcely
contain ourselves)

not a cough,
        not a shuffle,
his stance pivotal

above the excited young
        clustered around him
in all our promise,

focused with shining faces
        on the place of measurement itself,
pointing, like children.

Not a stir,
    not a breath,
there at the heart of old Vienna.

   *

Overtures and alliances.
    White gloves advance,
decorated bellies retire

down mirrored halls.
    Entente. Volte face.
And seize your partner.

And it's off to the muttonchop slaughter.
    Belted and buttoned brilliant hosts
march to their places line abreast,

bannerets fluttering among their pikes,
    kettledrums beating to match their boots
and, where they halt, to match their pulse,

on a field that will live for ever in glory,
    often as not beside some river,
rivers being natural boundaries

and offering certain useful features
    when the awful day is over.
We might search for harmony there

close up among
    the tangled woebegone
the morning after.

Or we might choose to listen
    down echoing and mirrored walls,
chandelier after trembling chandelier

to the vanishing point,
    with that infinite
imperial Ear

for Whom (a passionate amateur,
		Himself a gifted performer)
our most significant utterances

have been elicited from precisely this matter
		—in ominous drumrolls, slow marches
of tragic penetration,

in blaze of trumpets,
		unstoppable affirmations,
the logic of majesty.

For there are great iron entities
		afloat like towns erect on the water
with new murderous skills,

and there are thunderclouds gathered
		on our perimeter, and the Empire
turns once more toward its farrow.

*

And it is his last year, and the last time
		he is to introduce a new work to us,
and we can tell.

Was there ever one chasm closed
		but another opened
on our case

				—however the medium,
		blood-bearing in itself,
might seem temperate and good?

Or our Music Master
		fold the terms of the curse
back upon itself

in sensible figures in the air
		so the blood might beat at our temples
with the pulse of order

(let it be
        only even as
the work passed)

as though our 'celestial companions'
        shivering all about us in the night
were to slip their mythic roles

and disclose themselves
        with sudden ease as one,
solved in a single figure: The Elect,

a Man and a Woman, the minutiae
        of their breathings together
answered in great glittering systems,

with his hatchet face and rigid rod
        thrown against the blazing heart
in a happy ending.

While as to a beginning
        it is hard to see past
our first parent

patented on his Chapel ceiling
        propped on an elbow,
a languid and burly young man

with everything limply on show,
        and a little out of condition,
finger to finger with God the Father,

the Latter afloat toward him
        with the nub of the matter displaced
in a fold of His purple shift.

Yet enough, surely to that Patriarch-Mother
        —ending or beginning—
that from such thoughts forth

it was only in the excesses of our minds and art
    that we need to undergo
the outrage we appear to find essential.

Allowing always
    for that outrageous rummaging,
breath stopped, pulse paused

in its withheld double dark beat,
    with forces narrowed
in each chosen other.

*

For what shall it profit a white gloved
    and glittering bellied elder
puffed sideways at the camera

that mile after drowsy mile
    with bell towers and canals of still water
and deep green laneways doped with living flesh

and town squares cluttered with coffee tables
    and brown brick alleyways teeming
with the ignorant and able young

should darken against themselves,
    and iron animals clamber
in staggered series

up out of the creases and folds
    in our spirits onto dry land
and turn it to mud under us,

and drums burst in ditches at our feet
    and the ghosts of pikes
stutter all around us

and bannerets of our own selves
    dangle on wires along
irregular rivers of our own making,

so that upon a fixed hour
        a long horn will honk
and the field is his or another's

and ground breezes pick their ways
        across its brimming puddles
and into its unnatural lairs?

There are photographs
        of the sudden peace:
the late enemies together like family groups

half leaning against one another.
        There is a heavy boot in one
actually standing on a fallen hand.

Intermezzo

Munich
—December 1914

To——

My dear Sir, and Warrior,
        I was filled with inadequacy and shame
when they told me you had marched away.

I have set my mind now
        —since I can offer nothing else—
to the service of the German cause.

For I believe it is important
        to articulate and ennoble these happenings
and give them meaning.

How will it all end?
        The anxiety, the curiosity,
are immense. But is there not

a joy in the curiosity?
That all things will be made new
by this profound and powerful event

and the German people emerge from it
stronger and prouder,
freer and happier?

Grant it may be so.
All hail and victory,
my dear Herr Doktor.

I pray your Christmas
will have a strange beauty
in these harsh circumstances.

I take your hand in friendship
and remain
gratefully yours,

T— M—

2

A step forward and a lesser
step back, the baton withdrawn.
A timed excision.

'Glockenspiel!'
The bony left fingers
prise it open.

'Tuba! Double basses!'
There is a prolonged emptying
of the writhing contents.

'Trumpets and drenching strings!'
Is there anything quite like
getting to the root?

Dolce . . . He reaches
      for something soothing.
His shoulders sag for a bar of silence.

But why is there no ease?
      For something magnuscule has been accomplished;
the entities that made it possible

are locked together still;
      they have not even
begun to look at one another.

He stirs on his pinnacle.
      He is summoning
the ghost of a double beat,

a felt weight on the ear,
      fishchill,
a remote stink

from the depths,
      news ascending
speechless from a lower cold

where the senses have no function.
      It assumes a body.
It is a brute bobbin

throwing a hard shade
      backward and down,
and spearing upward

with dead eye and hacked downlaugh
      and slope of hide
shimmering with instincts

toward a glitter of tiny voices
      whispering among themselves:
I am! I am!

*

And indeed you are
— teeming everywhere
with your aches and needs

along our bloody passageways
knocking against one another
in neverending fuss

as if there were no matching
and more than matching
voracious peace.

Mind minnows
with flickering
intelligence-flecks for faces;

carrion swarming to fill
every pulse passing
in unsureness or error;

now, before we suffer Her
to gather us once more
into Her farewell and for ever,

I wag this pale finger
down among you
in promise

(fuss
propped upon promise
implying purpose,

waste
a part of the process,
implying life):

that there is an outer carrion
bone-walking in a dream bedlam,
half lit, idling

in foul units,
        circling our furthest reach
with a refusing snarl,

and that from even this matter
        (as of man's head rammed against stone
and woman a mad animal)

we might yet make a gavotte
        to feed
that everlasting Ear.

*

It is absolutely Heavenly:
        the very first morning.
All the strings are agreed.

Our couple are taking the air
        by the sea side,
content in their own sweet silence,

at arm's length
        —it is ocean and earth
that are touching.

In the faded photo the sea surface
        is sheer silver,
not one rock

to break the abstract
        mathematics of the brine,
or that a temptress

might clamber up
        and slither onto
to try out a throaty call.

She accompanies him
        on the ribbed and running salt sand,
skirted full length,

stamped blank
        under her black broad-brimmed hat,
coupling her attentive shadow with his

as he strolls in his tight trousers,
        jabbing sandworms and brooding
how to respond,

how to admire the solid beloved.
        Morning . . .
A shimmering calm . . .

A little wind
        disturbing what there is of hair . . .
Very well.

Let the Fall begin,
        the whole wide
landscape descend gently

—the open air
        a single throat
thrown wide

in a gasp of
        alarm and praise—
and a portal close.

And there ought to be
        a good deal of wandering
and seeking for peace

and desire of one kind and another,
        with the throat employed
for its own lovely sake

in moving utterances
        made of the simplest poetry.
Good man-made matter

is best for our design:
        forest murmurs; a tired horseman
drinking in friendship and farewell;

voices blurred in longing;
        renewal in Beauty;
Earth's pale flowers blossoming

in a distance turning to pure light
        shining blue
for ever and for ever.

And central to the Song's force
        an awareness
(in the actual motions of the mouth,

the intimacy of
        its necessary movements)
of her two nutrient smiles:

the one with lips pouted soft
        in half wet love
in earnest of

that other,
        dwelling upon itself for ever,
her vertical smile.

Coda

Nine are the enabling elements
        in the higher crafts
and the greatest of these is Luck.

I lift my
        baton and my
trousers fall.

. . . the perfection of their art seems to lie in their concealing it, as if 'it were the better for being hidden. An art revealed brings shame.' Hence it happens that the very things that afford unspeakable delight to the minds of those who have a fine perception and can penetrate carefully to the secrets of the art, bore, rather than delight, those who have no such perception—who look without seeing, and hear without being able to understand. When the audience is unsympathetic they succeed only in causing boredom with what appears to be but confused and disordered noise . . .

—Giraldus Cambrensis, on Irish music

Entrance

Crows scoured the wet evening clean
above our heads.

Two languages interchanged.

We came to a halt
with our half-certainties:

that love is to clasp simply,
question fiercely;

and the artistic act . . .
long library bodies, their pens
distinct against the sinking sun.

Native Wisdom

We leaned against the rain-spitted
wind
and got the gate open
into the churchyard.

A flat roof of stone
lay like a tongue
in the coarse grass.

Medals and beads and bits of mirror
by the hooded well,
a clip shimmering in the water,
the pious litter gave witness.

A crow scuffled in the hedge
and floated out with a dark groan
toward the church tower,
and flapped onto the parapet:

I am native born in this place.
I have knowledge of flesh and blood.
Come and buy.

Half way up the church wall
the Black Robber
stretched out his neck and stared:

Give ear to him and he will fill it
with nothing but white rubbish.
I am native born in your foul deeds.
Good and evil come and buy.

On an oval stone set over the window
she crossed her thin arms downward
and offered her opened self:

This swallows them both
and all the questions.
Here you are native born.
Yes and no come here and buy.

Rough stones stood everywhere
tilted in a soil thick with re-burials,
with a hole half open
in the ground at the foot of one of them
like a mouth:

I am born again in the spirit. So shall you be.
Love is all or nothing.
Come and buy.

Harmonies

Seamus of the Smart Suit, box player,
made signals to us across the grass tussocks and graves
the day we all came down from Cork
to commemorate our musical friend.

By Gobnait's sculpted lump
—a slab of a woman on a frieze of stone buds
and the locked bodies of bees—
he struggled in his nose with English,

showing the Holy Stations and instructing
with rigid finger and embarrassed snorts,
his box squeezed shut back in the house
with Mairtín's pipes and the pair of fiddles,

the same instruments, ranging together
in natural sweetness, with a many-sounded
and single voice, that gave Iohannes Scotus
—Eriugena, and instructing the known world—

his harmonious certainty: that the world's parts,
ill-fitted in their stresses and their pains,
will combine at last in polyphonic sweet-breathing union
and all created Nature ascend like joined angels,

limbs and bodies departing the touch of Earth
static in a dance of return, all Mankind
gathered stunned at the world's edge
silent in a choir of understanding.

The Furnace

Imperishable creatures
returning into God's light.
A resurrection, not a vanishing.

Intensifying, as iron
melts in the furnace
—intensified into flowing fire,

aching for a containing Shape.
Eriugena's notion matching
my half-baked, bodily own,

who have
consigned my designing will
stonily to your flames

and will turn again toward the same furnace
that melted the union of our will
to ineffable zero

how many times in its radiant clasp
(a cancellation
certainly speechless for a minute or two)

in token of the Union and the Light.
Until gender returned
and we were made two again

Male and Female
in punishment for Man's will
and reminded of our Fall.

In token of which
I plant this dry kiss
in your rain-wet hair.

The Dance

It is the staling music of memory
has brought us nosing once more
around our forgotten young hero

and his high-spirited doings.
Grieving solos fade
and twine on echoes of each other

down the shallow valley:
his own voices,
divided against themselves.

His spirit, in one piece still
(just for a little while,
and only just)

is cavorting in answer
all brains and bare feet
along the scruffy skyline,

stepping the parish boundary
in goodbye
and beckoning with a comical thumb

up over the edge:
Come and buy
my terrible new capabilities . . .

The little plants shivering
green and pale on the far slope
in a breeze out of the Next Testament,

unplaceable, familiar smells
stealing among the goats'
dainty, unbothered feet.

And there would be no sign
if we tried to follow
his shifting rhythms,

the throaty piping,
the dry taps fractured on the drum skin,
the delicate new hooves

on approval, slithering to the beat
down out of sight
into the stony places.

The Land of Loss

Nothing certain of this world,
Iohannes teaches,
except for certain impediments
we might carry with ourselves:

our legs bound, for our failure
to walk in the Divine Law;
our hands hindered, for their hesitation
in virtuous deeds;

and it grows dark and we stumble
in gathering ignorance
in a land of loss
and unfulfillable desire.

He himself was driven out of France
and half way home for heresy.

He taught in the Abbey at Malmesbury
and died there at his students' hands.

They stabbed him with their pens
because he made them think.

Exit

Lidless, lipless, opensocketed
and dumb with suspended understanding,
waiting for the Day,

our best evidence
is aligned all about under us,
their figures finished.

The dance is at our own feet.
Give me your hand.
A careful step

together over that outstuck
tongue, and shut this gate
in God's name

behind us, once and for all.
And reach me my weapon
in the goat-grey light.

ST CATHERINE'S CLOCK (1987)

The whole terrace
slammed shut.
I inhaled the granite lamplight,
divining the energies of the prowler.

A window opposite, close up.
In a corner, a half stooped image
focused on the intimacy
of the flesh of the left arm.

The fingers of the right hand are set
in a scribal act on the skin:
a gloss, simple and swift as thought,
is planted there.

The point uplifted,
wet with understanding,
he leans his head a moment
against the glass.

      I see.

Thomas Street at the first hour.

The clock
on the squat front of St Catherine's
settled a gilded point
up soundless into place.

1803

After the engraving by George Cruikshank

Lord Kilwarden, genuflected
prim and upset outside his carriage door,
thrown back rhetorical

among a pack of hatted simians,
their snouted malice gathered
into the pike-point entering his front.

His two coachmen
picked, like his horses, from a finer breed
register extremes of shocked distress.

Somewhere a nephew,
Mr Richard Wolfe, is fallen
and spilling his share of blood and matter.

From a non-contemporary nationalist artist's impression

And Robert Emmet on the scaffold high,
as close as possible to the site of the outrage,
is dropped from his brief height

into a grove of redcoats
mounted with their rumps
toward a horrified populace.

The torch of friendship and the lamp of life
extinguished, his race finished,
the idol of his soul offered up,

sacrificed on the altar of truth and liberty,
awaiting the cold honours of the grave,
requiring only the charity of silence,

he has done.
The sentence pronounced in the usual form,
he has bowed and retired.

The pasty head is separated and brandished aloft,
the dead forehead with the black wet lock
turned toward the Fountain.

1792

Jas. Malton, del.

At the drink shop by the Church corner
two horsemen are greeting,
their mounts brow to brow.

In the background
some activity about the water fountain:
a pair of children or dwarfs,

a man and woman with buckets,
a couple of mongrels
worrying the genitals out of each other.

Centre, barefoot,
bowed in aged rags to the earth,
a hag

toils across the street
on her battered business,
a drained backside

turned toward St Catherine;
everybody, even those
most near, turned away.

Right foreground, a shade waits for her
humped man-shaped against a dark cart
with whipstaff upright.

Set down to one side
by unconcerned fingers, a solitary redcoat
is handling the entire matter.

Past the Watch House and Watling Street
beyond St James's Gate, a pale blue
divides downhill into thin air

on a distant dream
of Bow Lane
and Basin Lane.

1938

Two red-and-black matched silky-decorated
tin boxes out of India
fit beside each other behind her
up on the tea shelf, behind her head.

The shoulders of the black iron-flowered
weighing-scales on the counter
balance, embossed, across the socket-top of the stand.
The brass plates hang, equal, in their chains.

Round ounce weights
and multiples and little
black fractions nestle
on one another against the base.

Her knuckles and waxy nails took hard hold
of the counter-lid.
She had a fat sugar sack,
with the twiny neck rolled back,

tucked in against her high stool
and the black boot laced up
under her skirt and the black beads
hanging down over her brown apron.

In on a dark shelf
on the way into the back
she had the goose eggs from down the country,
green and big, the fill of your palm.

*

Aunty Gertie shuffled
across the scullery. She had
big slippers and a slow bum.

Little Uncle Ned was always in and out
grinning at her. (Uncle Larry said
she could stick him in her pocket.)

She could let a long belch
up her neck, like a noise
coming up out of a jug.

*

I was inside in the back room
up on the bed with a rolled-up newspaper
at the holy picture, killing flies.

The whole bed
gave when I moved across it
in the pillow smell.

There was one on the glass
on the Sacred Heart's face,
with the black little pointed head

and dead eyes
looking everywhere.
It kept twining and wiping its thin paws.

273

But somebody in the other room
shouted: 'Go on out
and tell your Aunty Cis we want her'

and it disappeared, and started flying
up with the others around and around
at angles under the bulb.

*

Sometimes some of the aunts
wouldn't talk for weeks,
in a bad temper after passing remarks.

They chewed their teeth
and passed each other by
with their glasses and stiff faces.

But some of them would keep muttering
together in the middle room.
And then someone one day suddenly

would laugh up out of her throat,
and all the put-on pain and the high snout
would go out of their stares.

*

Up the bright road starting toward Naas
with the line of new houses
going up the long hill
into the country

near the big white Chapel
with the two spires
towering up off the front wall
full of arches and holy figures and stone flowers

we turned off into a hidden
street of brown houses
down to a door in the quietest corner
to visit our best cousins,

older, handsome boys, all with fine teeth,
all three of them doing well,
two of them always
understanding and good.

*

We shouted everywhere at one another
—even in whispers, out over the river brink,

holding onto the rushes, hardly breathing
down through our shadows into the water

for the sign of a striped perch pretending
among the reeds or sheltering against the bank,

to see it move, and drop a stone in
scattering our faces.

*

The Night crept
among our chalk signs on the path
and trickled into the shores.

The moon hung round and silver
out over the empty Back
between the backs of the people's houses

where we piled the rubbish up
on the clay in the dark
and set it on fire and talked into the flames

and skipped around in wickedness
with no mercy to the weak or the fat
or the witless or the half blind.

*

I have struggled, hand
over hand,
in the savage dance.

I have lain inert, the flesh in nightmare,
eating and eaten,
with eyes wide open.

The balm of a clouded breast . . .
The musk of a stocking rolled down
over her pale knee beside the fire-place.

Then left by myself
sitting up in the fire shadows,
little fingertip touches

flickering reddened
over my picture book.
I let them,

and let it fall after a while
and the security of love
found a place in my marrow.

A little boy, some kind of an uncertain
shade, started trying to get up
with wings dragging.

Then upright in beauty,
his pinions touched with the red firelight.
He turned his golden head.

But when I woke again it was all restless
with the stare of love's hatred
and you that know well and will not know

and ill-will spitting
casual at the street corner, ignorant
born and bred.

And I have sat solitary
outside, on the low window-sill,
a brutal nail nagging out of nowhere.

*

Sometimes it sounded like she was giving out
but she was really minding us.

I know I was not bold
even if I did terrible things.

I was not a barefaced liar
and never went with the gets down the street.

I was always dressed properly,
and minded my brother.

One night we scrounged up together
and felt the little eggs in each other.

And I always remembered
who and what I am.

Grand Canal Place,
    at the second hour.
Live lights on oiled water
    in the terminus harbour.

Not fifty yards from here
she took the certificate
and slapped it down on the table.
It took that to shut them up.

Kathleen was very good
and Matty kindness itself.
With three sons of their own
they put her up for the birth.

Nurse Fitzsimons looked after her
out of the long bag. She was very fat
and looked after the whole neighbourhood
for twenty years afterwards.

*

His voice, empty and old,
came around to it more than once:
something about the family
he had to tell me sometime.

A dead voice now
in my ear: You can be certain
from your own cold certainties
that you are a son of hers.

But you would have to try
very far under my feeble force
to find anything more
than a passing kind of doggedness.

Closer than a brother
(born of the same woman,
face down face up to her fondness,
and a quiet brutal other

closer than a brother)
look for the dimpled smile
empty of understanding
that will tell you the rest of it.

I leave you a few faint questions
and good and bad example
and things I have not told you,
and who and what you are.

*

Bridie, the next and youngest,
the musical one of the family,
was hardly like an aunt at all,

bright and sharp, so unlucky
with her first love lost or dead
in Rio de Janeiro.

She knelt down quickly beside me
with her handbag and her schoolteacher's smile
for a hurried hug and goodbye,

the pair of us so alike,
everybody agreed,
wherever we got our brains.

Thomas Street.
As far as we can reach.
Turning a night face

and thin hair feeling the wet
from the Fountain
and some that are most near.

A modest bloody little trickle
is spilling this way and that
from the foot of the ghost of the scaffold

inching to the left,
starting down with the hill slope,
sensing the possibility of direction

—ghost handkerchiefs
dipped with tears, in communion,
in its course—

and sensing the far-off
impossible magnificat: a river
coiling its potent flood

between high block walls,
carrying a brand new soul
struggling with wet wings

to flourish a while in freedom
on the surface of our recollection
—not anchored in our angry hearts—

till it come to some more friendly port
to give it shelter against the heavy storms
with which it is buffeted.

Long-lost, a second-last letter,
written almost in his own tears,
was found years afterward
in the stuffing of a sofa.

*

On the right,
up in the slatted turret,
a tooth on the big measuring
wheel

re-engaged,
protestant,
inch by inch.

1740

About the third hour.

Ahead, at the other end
of the darkened market place
a figure crossed over

out of Francis Street
reading the ground, all dressed up
in black, like a madwoman.

Enough
is enough:
poring over that organic pot.

I knuckled my eyes. Their drying jellies
answered with speckles and images.
I leaned back and stretched

and embraced all
this hearth and home
echoing with the ghosts

of prides and joys,
bicycles and holy terrors,
our grown and scattered loves.

And all this place
where, it occurs to me,
I never want to be anywhere else.

Where the elements conspire.
Which is not to say
serenity and the interplay of friends

but the brick walls
of this sagging district, against which
it alerts me to knock my head.

With a scruffy nineteenth-century
history of half-finished
colonials and upstarts. Still with us.

Catholic Action next door:
the double look
over the half curtain;

social workers herding their problems
in off the street
with snooker cues and rosary beads;

Knights of Mercedes and the naked bulb
parked at large along both paths
in witness that the poor are being given a party.

With a half charm,
half gracious, spacious,
and a miscellaneous vigour.

Sniffed at. Our neighbourhood developer
thinking big in his soiled crombie.
The rodent element bidding out.

Invisible speculators, urinal architects,
and the Corporation flourishing their documents
in potent compliant dance

—planners of the wiped slate
labouring painstaking over a bungled city
to turn it into a zoo:

Southward from Fatima Mansions into the foothills;
Northward past our twinned experimental
concrete piss-towers for the underprivileged;

and at the heart, where the river runs
through Viking ghosts at every tide
by a set of shadow structures

that our city fathers, fumbling in their shadow budget,
beheld in vision for a while,
pulverising until the cash failed,

laying flat an enduring monument to themselves,
an office car park sunk deep in history.
May their sewers blast under them!

A sluggish creature
and difficult to house-train,
it spatters its own nest.

Dirty money gives dirty access.
And we were the generation
of positive disgrace.

And I want to throw my pen down.
And I want to throw my self down
and hang loose over some vault of peace.

Bright gulls, gracefully idling
in the blue and wholesome heights
above our aerials;

fatted magpie
big and bold
in the apple shade;

grey maggot, succulent
underfoot, inexorable
on your invisible way;

O green ash branches
whispering
against the sunny masonry;

Ah! baby spider
so swift
on the painted sill.

Fellow citizens! I embrace
your grasping manners, your natural behaviour,
as we thrive together for an instant.

And those also, friends and others,
of whose presences, deteriorating
here, there and elsewhere

I am acutely aware.
Here's a hug while the mood is on me.
Take your places around my table

one last time together.
Settling yourselves carefully,
startled you are on our list.

Uneasy. Delighted
if only there had been
a little more notice.

And let us not be bound by precedent.
We shall certainly need
an additional table or two.

*

The moment is at hand.
Take one another
and eat.

You, peremptory and commanding so long ago,
that so swiftly and methodically
discovered your limits.

You, so hesitant, so soon presumptuous,
urgent and confiding, breathing close
about nothing.

You, insistent, weak-smiling,
employing tedium to persuade,
vanishing when satisfied.

You, capering, predatory, inexhaustible in ideas,
the one thing certain
we will never know what was on your mind.

You with your bedtime mug of disappointment
—the loser in every struggle;
always on the right side.

You, flushed with bonhomie
but serious on the question of expenses;
always first with the bad news.

You, elbowing your way in,
out of your depth,
clumsy and comical, but determined;

surfacing long afterwards
in the Southern suburbs,
doing well, steering clear.

You, ageing in your junior grade,
applying your rules of thumb
with emphasis and ease.

You, managing the marginal cases
at your careworn table.
Keeping the fees flowing.

And you, all smiles on the formal floor,
muscling past the ladies
to get at the archbishop;

dedicated and purposeful,
you silenced us
with your skills in analysis,

excited us
with your direct methods,
and were startled with us at the result.

You, in morose inadequacy,
settling your contemporaries in order of precedence,
denying what you still might: discern.

Discern process. You know that,
mangled by it. We are all participants
in a process that requires waste.

You that with an ear
for the cold fathoms of the self
whistled up the Song of our own Earth,

turned a spirit off the rocks
into a fire in the gut
and, in the final phase,

happy with our half attention,
became an entertainer
among the lesser gentry.

You, our hectoring pontifical hack,
changing carthorses in midstream,
educating yourself in public.

You, our grocer's curate,
busy a long time in the back room,
grinning up front suddenly among the special offers.

And you, lecturing off the cuff, from on high,
the index cards arranged
behind the soles of your hands:

The procedures of criticism are understood.
Work not amenable to those procedures
does not call for consideration.

Ending with a modest bow
as though you had
said something.

You, invoking a sort of universal
common sense about art
—not trying to outlaw *Finnegans Wake*

but more interested in finding
true art, that can work
for a lot of people fairly quickly.

And you, handling the market direct,
tangled in your keys, uproarious,
but serious behind all the fun,

an artist to your elbow tips.
Forgotten, your past master,
your training like an animal.

And you. Fiddler with the pale eyebrows
and the holy water for blood,
your fingers flying in the last movement.

But give us a kiss.
For we are going somewhere,
and need every scrap of good.

Though only of good.
A stiff midfinger
in stern warning,

remembering one unnatural,
saddled with a womb, to whom
the organic was intolerable.

And one hugging her grey stare in the
morning,
waiting while her acid came to the boil,
stark staring sober.

One swift-mounted and commanding in the saddle
—tight-hammed at the kill,
ham-fisted at the inner table:

We have it all together.
It looks good.
The Blue Nun is on me.

And one withered and erect, satisfied
that poetry is anything extruded in pentameter,
recalling his first Catholics with amusement

—Brendan, Fergus, Cuchulainn . . .
Your views on the just society?
The eyes and the lips narrow.

And you, our activist commentator,
descending on London and the serious papers
with a bundle of dirty linen

ironed across your arm,
your briefcase full of applied literature
—baulked in Redmondite bafflement at human behaviour,

but complaining so melodiously
we could forgive you
almost anything.

*

The world laid low
and the wind blew like a dust
Alexander, Caesar, and all their followers.

Tara is grass;
and look how it stands with Troy . . .
And we were the generation also of privilege

to have seen the vitals of Empire tied off
in a knot of the cruel and comic.
Not to misunderstand

—the English are a fine people
in their proper place.
And two that circumstance saddled with each other

might have turned out something less like
the bully marriage next door
with the delph dancing off the wall

but the Creator's Anti-Christ was at Him.
And remember we are dealing with the slow to learn
whose fathers, wiping the blood up after their efforts,

fought the wrong civil war.
                              A modest proposal:
Everything West of the Shannon,

women and children included,
to be declared fair game.
Helicopters, rifles and night-glasses permitted.

The natives to have explosive
and ambush and man-trap privileges.
Unparalleled sport

and in the tradition
—the contemporary manifestation
of an evolving reality.

*

And he said,
Have love for one another
as I have loved the lot of you.

Now let us lift our thoughts
to our holy distracted Mother
torn between two stools.

Patroness of the manageable Catholic
that can twist on a threepenny bit;
and of the more difficult Protestant

twisting in the other direction
and interested more in property;
Thou that smilest however

on the pious of both persuasions
closest to the sources of supply,
guide us and save.

*

Enough.
That there is more spleen
than good sense in all of this, I admit

—and back to the Encyclopaedia I go.
Diderot, my hand upon it.
The pen writhed

and moved under my thumb
and dipped again
in its organic pot.

There are established personal places
that receive our lives' heat
and adapt in their mass, like stone.

These absorb in their changes
the radiance of change in us,
and give it back

to the darkness of our understanding,
directionless
into the returning cold.

Apostle of Hope

A greeting, and thanks, from this sick place
—our half-blind watch tower watching us
across the empty market square,
a squad of baby-looking troops
with deadly undernourished faces
waltzing across the cracked cement,
kneeling and posing with their guns.
Our polite faces packed with hate.

I won't forget your lair of a town.
That business breakfast there beside us,
their worried flashy expedients
for bringing life to the market centre.
At night, on our own, when the streets emptied,
the terrible number of waifs we met
in a silence of the stunned. The process
as it hath shown its waste to you.

Above all, lifted up on high,
enlarged by local enterprise,
Man the Measure cruciforked
upon His wheel, jacked up erect,
splayed like a target against the grey,
smooth as an ad. Grossness uprisen.
Godforsaken.

                    Forgive. Forgive.

The Impulse, ineradicable,
labours into life. Scrutiny;
manipulation toward some kind
of understanding; toward the Good.
The Process as it hath revealed
its Waste on high.

                    Let our hate reach that.

Seven

Will you dance at my doorway,
        perch at my porch?
Hurry darling,
        myriads in me demand it.

I flapped out haphazard
        across a glowing glade,
weightless, made of gauze,
        all the colours of the rainbow,

settled on a nodding
        solitary stem,
folded my wings
        and passed for a flower.

*

Foxglove and their faded flames nodded
down an alley of the greenwood shade.
A snapping fox shifted from doubt to doubt.

Steel carrion eyes
stared from a sharp midnight roof
above the empty square.

The leather claws
tightened on a stone face,
strengthening their hold with black nails.

*

Our thoughts touched in waking,
holding her live underarm,
honest hand on a tender tit.

A shadow of fumbled assent
with hand on uneasy heart,
in the fragrance of arm and throat.

A pigeon repeated its elaborate, brainless murmur.
The bedroom curtain inhaled
and filled with light.

*

In the name of the Father
all force

in the name of the spirit
gland of matter
blind staring bowel of being

in the name of the senses
ordered out
in their binary responding groves

deign, O crushed lips, pursed
in the woman dark
where'er you walk

to separate
beneath his kiss.

*

Seven.
A cloud shadow advanced
over the young barley

across the neighbouring fields,
and darkened the pair of cars
parked ill-matched in the yard.

Rituals of Departure

It is a misery, beloved friends, and my last wish.
But let us find what ease we can.
(Melancholy, retiring with her finger to our lips.)

*

We came out with the last suitcases strapped
and nothing left to say
onto the driveway under the high red oaks.

The children seen to and strapped in.
Speechless, and taking us by surprise
with their tears.

Our wagon turned away from the West.

*

And remember the detailed care you have had here.
And the love. And the other rituals of departure,
their ashes dying along our path.

Brothers in the Craft

In the creative generations there is often
a conspiracy of the mature and the brilliant young;
a taking in hand, in hopes of a handing on.

In the elder, an impulse against that settled state
when the elements work in balance against each other
in worn stability, no longer questioned;

to borrow something out of the restlessnesses
of the half ready, confide an ethereal itch
into new, committed fingers.

                            In the other,
a self-elect asking only to watch
—even be let hold something—the imbalance of growth.

These settle in the medium in their turn,
a part of the lasting colour of the work
taken from the early accidental particulars.

Again and again, in the Fifties, 'we' attended
Austin Clarke. He murmured in mild malice
and directed his knife-glance curiously amongst us.

Out in the dark, on a tree branch near the Bridge,
the animus of Yeats perched.
                            Another part of the City,
Tonio Kroeger, malodorous, prowled Inchicore.

In Memory

1
You were silver-quiffed and tall
and smiling above us in public,
formal and at ease. Established.
Introducing I have forgotten what.

It is you I remember.
Authoritative, from the Department.
Published recently, and discussed.
Managing both careers.

The audience, mainly literary,
stood about, interested
in what was to come. But we
were gathered at your feet.

2

The years passed. Our group broke up.
The character of our generation
emerged, with the fulfilment
and the failure of early promise,

with achievement in surprising places,
and one startling success
revealing a sagacity and a scope
undreamed of at the time.

Some left the country, or disappeared
as though they had never been.
Others stayed in irregular contact
our conversations growing more general.

3

A few assembled lately
on a miserable occasion.
We found each other in a crowd
from the intervening years,

familiar and unfamiliar faces,
acquaintances and strangers,
friends from later interests.
An unpleasantness here and there

—one, quiet-spoken and confiding,
not to be trusted again;
one nursing an old dispute
and able behind the scenes.

The narrow face of envy.
Hardness of heart. Self.
False witness. The irreducible
malice and greed of the species.

*

We stood near the older trees
—your box, massive and pale,
waiting on a pile of clay.
With what you were taking with you.

And leaving. The memory
of a gentle self, affronted
by the unmanageable,
aroused and self-devouring.

I walked away, along a file
of long-established graves,
remembering our last meeting.
You, overcoated and withdrawn,

sitting beside the fire
after another death.
Violent. One of yours,
inheriting your luck.

And I, making my way across
and settling at your side.
You starting a conversation
out of another time.

When I turned around to go back
it was a while before I discovered
our people among the others
—everybody everywhere with white hair.

Dura Mater

1

A potato smell came out from the kitchen door,
and a saucepan smell, with a piece of meat boiling.

She came along the passage in her slippers
with a fuzz of navy hair, and her long nails
held out wet out of the washing water.

Come here to me. Come here to me, my own son.

Stiff necked, she put up her pursed mouth
at her grown young—whatever idea she had of it
in there behind the ill temper in her eyes.

Will you look at him. How do you stick him at all.

And offered, and withdrew, a Cupid's Bow puckered,
closed lids, a cheek of withered silk,
the little smell of her hairline powdered over.

2

The withheld kiss returned
onto her stone forehead. Dura Mater.

To take it, a seal on her stone will,
in under the screwed lid.

3

He came out, stooping forward
with hands held down before him
still joined in the gesture of prayer,
his feet heavy but employed with care.

The sides of hair receding around his scalp
were moistened and dyed dark,
the face downcast,
the eyes soft but emphatic.

The air was filled with music.

*

He stepped into the funeral coach outside,
with quick irritated hand gestures
repeated without meaning,
a motiveless urging in the uplifted, inviting voice.

4

I entered the lobby at the hour appointed,
a crowded place, low-ceilinged and obscure.
I found the place to wait, beside a great
illuminated plant in a stone pot.

Sudden and silent, he was there beside me.

I have come to speak with him, after so long,
because I have a question. But first to our places.
The instruments to hand on either side,
seated opposed, we settled down and ate.

I put the question. Certainly. Of course.
I am sorry you had to ask. There should be something
next week in the post, or the week after.
I'll see to that. And we must keep in touch.

Night Conference, Wood Quay: 6 June 1979

Our iron drum of timbers blazed and sparked
in rusty tatters at the mouth of the shed,
apples and bread and bottles of milk flickering.

'. . . We have a truce. They have made every mistake.
There are only a few thugs . . .' A voice rasped:
'You couldn't trust their oath.' A tired growl: hand-clapping.

The half-dug pits and night drains brimmed with matter.
A high hook hung from the dark: the swift crane locked
—and its steel spider brain—by our mental force.

*

Where are they, looking down. At what window.
Visages of rapine, outside our circle of light.
Their talk done. The white-cuffed marauders.

At the Western Ocean's Edge

Hero as liberator. There is also
the warrior marked by Fate, who overmasters
every enemy in the known world
until the elements reveal themselves.
And one, finding the foe inside his head,
who turned the struggle outward, against the sea.

Yeats discovered him through Lady Gregory,
and found him helpful as a second shadow
in his own sour duel with the middle classes.
He grew to know him well in his own right
—mental strife; renewal in reverse;
emotional response; the revelation.

Aogan O Rathaille felt their forces meeting
at the Western ocean's edge
—the energy of chaos and a shaping
counter-energy in throes of balance;
the gale wailing inland off the water
arousing a voice responding in his head,

storming back at the waves with their own force
in a posture of refusal, beggar rags
in tatters in a tempest of particulars.
A battered figure.
                              Any force remaining
held on waves of threat inside the mind.

As who can not confirm, that set his face
beyond the ninth shadow, into dead calm.
Dame Kindness, her bowels torn.
The stranger waiting on the steel horizon.

A Portrait of the Artist

We might have guessed it would end in argument
and the personal. The cool, acid exchanges
in the small hours, hoarse in the hall:
An architect is an artist! His first duty is beauty!
Finding our way down the steps;
walking up the terrace in relief.

A pair of figures the other side of the Canal.

*

*They had reached the canal bridge
and, turning from their course . . .*
continued, locked in argument.
                                        About there.

One, nagging beauty to her place
among the senses. And the fool
lending a quick, inadequate ear:
But what is beauty.

A jewel of process.
The fugitive held fast, exact in its accident

My hands framed your throat in the night air.

*

A car prowled across the Bridge
and halted, then turned in a slow curve
under the lamp back over the Canal
with another following on its track,
the rear lights pulsing rose.

305

A pair of shades. One, in a short skirt,
stirred herself; the other, in black leatherette,
waited back against the railings,
the tip of her cigarette red. Her eyes
and her oyster mouth wet to my thoughts.

Administrator

We knew him first as a pious reputation,
businesslike, a new breed in the neighbourhood.
Stationed out among the people. Accustomed
to property and its management. Seldom seen.

He appeared once, in response to a complaint.
Entered the front hall, quietly discourteous,
suited in grey, easy to mistake
for a Protestant colleague;
and sat across the table, not really listening,
his response ready, looking past the speaker.

Our charges have certain needs. If these entail
annoyance for others that is unfortunate.
But we are there.
                    One lapse: a fumbled exit.

Then handed matters back to the lay staff.

Social Work

The meeting ended, and the delegates
moved off among themselves around the room.
I turned away to talk to a new neighbour.

A voice at my ear: 'I think we may give it up.'
A pair of furious Corporation officials
had stepped across to one of the high windows

with the social workers—the very Catholic doctor,
the house agent at his elbow, silver-haired—
and the parish priest, present as an observer.

The latter had chatted pleasantly before the meeting
but was otherwise quiet. He was speaking now
at the centre of the group, the others nodding.

The Stable

A loft, out of the market place,
of beams and whitened stone. Where the feed
was forked out, down to the Lane.

The ivy opposite, crept at last
over the date and initials painted
big and uneasy on the wall.
Where he kept the dray, half stacked with sacks.

O'Keeffe.
          Unbothered for forty years
he took the path from the stable door
back to the tap, and ran the water
into the bucket under his thumb.
He held the rim up spilling against
the teeth and the rubber lips of the horse
shifting its hooves in the wheaten stink.

Starting out, at the cross lane,
it smelled the water off the Canal,
and fidgetted with a creak of straps
—tossing its face and rearing back
in the black tackle, half in earnest.
Then settled down between the shafts.

When O'Keeffe got sick
the wife and the helpful son-in-law
manoeuvred it out for the last time.
She waited back in the stable, crying.
They both knew well the kind of hold
they were handing over with the key.

When O'Keeffe came out his every move
was new and deliberate, exercising
along the Canal as far as the Lane
and back again by Haddington Road.

We sat in the kitchen across from each other:
I said Three Pounds. He made it Five.
We shook hands and I wrote it down
—the cash to be left on the window sill
where he left the rent.
                              And he wasn't gone
a month when the local roughs were in.

Household Spirits

From somewhere underneath my window
a thrush flew across to Comers' wall
and hovered under the dripping creeper,

holding its speckled brown body
agitated in the air, pecking up
at a little black bunch of berries,

then darted
back across the Lane
out of sight.

With the red juice in his mouth
he is consulting
the cannibal committee downstairs,

come at our call up through Australia
to stand carved in inquiry
or hang from their hooks and rafters;

mongrel images shaped in wood
with a fluency like dung.
Collect of innocent evils—

grinning nude with ibis,
a squat goose extruding a skull,
a scaled midget glaring,

a fatuous-ferocious flat head
on edge, like an animal pat,
with muddied tongue outstuck,
no eyeball to no eyeball.

The Bell

The bell on Haddington Road rang,
a fumbled clang behind the flats.
Anderson calling to his neighbour.

Hauling down on the high rope,
announcing his iron absolutes
audible in Inchicore.

Disturbing the sanctuary lamp
—cup of blood, seed of light,
hanging down from their dark height.

The Back Lane

The long workroom, in a dead light
    and a brain and book odour, as it was left.
The book I came for was still open

at the title-page and the sharp
      elderly down-tasting profile.
Close it with one finger, and gather it up.

*

Outside, in the first night air,
      the double timber door scraped across
shut, under the wet vine.

I leaned back against the wood
      on serpent terms with Comers' cat
on the wall opposite, deadly in the open.

A black stain of new tar on the ground
      —shade that in the beginning
moved on the concrete.

And the remains of a cement mash
      emptied direct on the clay; revealing
the clumsiness of the telephone people,

the slovenliness of the City and its lesser works.
      Culpable ignorance, distinguishing Man
from the cat and the other animals.

I stirred a half brain of cauliflower
      with my foot, on wet paper
against the corrugated tin and the neglect next door.

The Moon had set.
      And the Plough, emblem of toil.
And my own sign had descended.

Three Corporation lamps lit the way
      along the wall to the far corner,
and I started down the middle of the Lane

with the book at my heart
>and the pen patted in its pocket.
Past stables and back gates

in various use and ruin:
>vegetable and mongrel smells, a scent of clay
and roots and spinster flesh.

*

It was something to do with this
>brought me looking for you at this hour.
Not anything to do with management or method

—prejudice veiled as justice, the particulars
>rearranged with a mathematical scowl;
or your childlike direct way with system.

But the smell of exit:
>the next,
>>and last, excitement.

With the simplest form imposed
>—three lamps brightening and embracing
and fading behind me in the dark.

As far as the cross lane,
>and out among your larger works, City Fathers,
into the world of waste.

*

I stopped at the junction
>in a first smell of water off the Canal,
and allowed myself a prayer, with open arms

—the right arm held up hanging empty,
>the left lifting my book;
with the wrists nailed back:

Lord, grant us a local watchfulness.
    Accept us into that minority
driven toward a totality of response,

and I will lower these arms
    and embrace what I find.
Embarrassed.

        Encountering my brother figure.
    —Startled likewise, in that posture
of seeming shyness, then glaring,

lips set and dark,
    hands down and averted
that have dipped in the same dish with mine.

But it was no one I knew,
    hurrying out onto the terrace,
the features withdrawn and set in shame.

The Stranger

Years ago, while we were settling in,
I saw him passing by this side of the Canal,
a clerk from somewhere in the area.

Then, more accustomed to the neighbourhood,
I noticed him the other side of the Bridge,
crossing over from Mount Street opposite

or turning away in the dark along the base
of the heavy-set terrace, back around the Church
with the little peppercanister cupola.

One evening, when our house was full of neighbours
met in upset, I was standing by the drapes
and saw his face outside, turned up to the light.

And once in Baggot Street I was talking with someone
when he passed with a word or two to the other, his face
arab up close. We smiled in antipathy.

In another time I might have put it down
to evil luck or early death—the Stranger
close upon our heels—and taken care.

But you and I were starting to deal already
with troubles any Stranger might desire.
Our minds in their teeming patterns died each night.

Once, at an upper window, at my desk,
with the photographs and cuttings pinned in fury
around the wall, and tacked across the blind,

I found a structure for my mess of angers,
lifted out of the school dark:
                              Distracted

one morning by a stream, in circumstances
of loveliness and quiet, not for him,
a poet sinks to the ground and hides his face

in harrowed sleep. A kindly beauty approaches,
unworldly, but familiar—one of us—
comforts his misery, and turns his thoughts

toward some theatrical hope . . .

                              He reawakens,
distracted still.

A simple form; adjusting
simply with the situation,
and open to local application; weakened

by repetition; ridiculed and renewed
at last in parody. My pen quickened
in a pulse of doggerel ease.

When I beheld him the other side of the road,
overacting, bowing with respect;
resuming his night patrol along the terrace.

Leaving my fingers stopped above the paper.

Departure Platforms

A swan erected in anger, stiffening his neck.
His cygnets were busy, pecking and paddling
grey-furred among the heaps of worn tyres
around the sunny dock in Portobello
—the Canal harbour they filled in years ago.

A sack floated, half sunk, against the bank
where the people from the new Canal Hotel
stepped onto their fat, fashionable barges.

*

A crowd of people came hurrying up the staircase.

A girl with thick spectacles entered
and looked around her, one leg kneeling
in a metal thing, turning back and forth
with practised movements. 'A knee-crutch', I whispered.

A woman stood a moment inside the gate
resting, in middle age, with a heavy suitcase,
her legs wrapped in reddened bandages.
'Look', I whispered. 'They are still bleeding.'

He laughed: 'They come to your call.'

The Last

Standing stone still on the path, with long pale chin
    under a broad-brimmed hat, and aged eyes
staring down Baggot Street across his stick.
    Jack Yeats. The last.

Upright, stately and blind, and hesitating
    solitary on the lavatory floor
after the Government meeting down the hall.
    De Valera. The last.

Memory of W. H. Auden

A tangle of concerns
above the dark channel of Baggot Street.
Jesus in History. Man and his Symbols.
Civilization Surprised in her Underwear.

Lost—turning away toward something—
with my claws picking at the paint
on the sill at an upper window.

When I saw a stone-bright dead light
move on their scribal pallor.
Not an earthly effect. But not imagined,
the chimneys and the slate roofs South to the hills
touched by the same.
                Swollen full
on high, a corpsegaze
imposed on a ghost of brilliance
staring down out of the Thirties
—rapt, radiant with vision and opinion,
flawed with the final furrows.
Secondary father, with cigarette.

Found—turning back into my den.
Your scarred regard bright on my shoulder,
my fingers finding their way
back about their business, with the taint upon them.

Better is an handful with quietness
than both hands full
with travail and vexation of spirit.

Better to leave now, and no more of this loving upset,
hate staining the door-jamb from a head possessed
—all things settled sour in their place,
my blind fingers forsaking your face.

Yet worst is the fool that foldeth his hands
and eateth his own flesh.

Madonna

Her high heels sounded nearer
in the aisle, tapping on the tiles.

She knelt beside me at the money-box
in the light of the candles,
under the Body with the woman feet.

Her head bowed. Her meat sweet.

*

She was busy, minding her hair
at the window, a long brushful held out.

Looking out at the night
and the light coming in
dead white off the street, and the shadow
invading our urinary privacy.

317

*

In concern and familiarity
it is done: our two awarenesses
narrowed into one point,
our piercing presences exchanged
in pleasantry and fright.

Our senses tired
and turning toward sleep,
our thoughts disordered
and lapped in fur,

your shoulder sleeping
distinct in my hand,
the tally of our encounters
reduced by one.

*

Cut and fold it open,
the thick orange, honey-coarse.
First blood: a saturated essence
tasted between the teeth.

I held the kettle out high
and emptied it
with a shrivelled hiss
boiling into the scalded pot.

A stubborn memory:
her tender, deliberate incursions.

Morning Coffee

1

We thought at first it was a body
rolling up with a blank belly onto the beach
the year our first-born babies died.

A big white earthenware vessel
settled staring up
open mouthed at us.

The first few who reached it
said they thought they caught
a smell of blood and milk.

Soon we were making up stories
about the First People
and telling them to our second born.

*

A loving little boy
        appeared on angel's wings
and showed his empty quiver.
        I filled it out of mine.

He vanished, but remembered:
        every dart
returning furious
        to my heart.

*

At a well beside the way
I alighted and put down
my lips to the water.

You, lifting your face
like a thirsty thing to mine,
I think I know you well:

of character retiring,
settled in your habits,
careful of your appearance;

with eyes open inward;
restless in disposition;
best left alone.

What matter if you seem
assured in your purpose
and animal commitment

but vague in direction
and effect on affairs?
Resolved on perfection

but soon indecisive?
We are all only pilgrims.
Travelling the night.

2

It was late, on a wet morning
at a side table,
the cup hot in my two hands,

my notes against the chair
with a few late cases
debating among themselves.

There were a few others sitting
around the long room.
One or two on each others' minds.

Outside, through the basement window,
there were feet hurrying at eye height
around the corner, through the rain.

The cobbles opened in a wide yard
out among the old buildings
—the one shop, the offices

up the tenement stone stairs—
then narrowed in a lane along by the Library
toward the car, still cooling.

I felt at my throat with thumb and finger.
The shaved leather.
                              An hour earlier

—standing stripped at the sink,
holding the affected wrist
too long under the scalding tap,
sharp with pain and pleasure . . .

I pushed the chair back;
the others upstairs starting to wonder.
And left my cup for the woman waiting.

Visiting Hour

The pale inner left arm pierced and withdrawn,
the sweat-heated pillow flattened under my neck,
          I lay and fingered my mental parts.

A draft stirred the red curtain: a figure
at the foot of the bed, observing like a brother.
          Not much trace of him before our trouble . . .

But I needed nothing there. They must be letting
anybody in. I lifted a ham
          in thoughtful ease. The curtain settled back.

The blood beating injected in the face.
The two tablets, bitten to a flour,
          melting in an aftertaste of coffee.

An aura like a cloud around the heart.
Memories intermixing, opening inward,
          and melting in the loins with a ghost of pleasure.

I turned away, toward the tall Victorian window.
And she was there, against the crimson drape.
    One thin hand out, denying,

the other pulling the lace back from her thigh
and the dark stocking with the darker border
    toward the pale motherly places:

the sac of flesh and fervour where we met
and nourished each other for a while.
    Mother, in your faded folds,

taking refreshment at my well of illness,
fragile in the smell of woodbine,
take my love back, into the medicine dark.

At the Head Table

The air grew dark with anger
toward the close of the celebration.
But remembering his purpose
he kept an even temper

thinking: I have devoted
my life, my entire career,
to the avoidance of affectation,
the way of entertainment

or the specialist response.
With always the same outcome.
Dislike. Misunderstanding.
But I will do what I can.

He rose, adjusting his garments,
lifted the lovely beaker
with the slim amphibian handles,
and turned toward the source of trouble.

'Madam. Your health. Your patience.
Unlock those furious arms,
or we who respect and love you
will have to take offence.

How often, like this evening,
we have sat and watched it happen.
Discussing the same subjects
from our settled points of view,

our cheer turning to bitterness
with one careless word,
and then the loaded silence,
staring straight ahead.

Oh for the simple wisdom
to learn by our experience!
I know from my daily labour
it is not too much to ask.

This lovely cup before us
—this piece before all others—
gave me the greatest trouble,
in impulse and idea

and management of material,
in all the fine requirements
that bring the craftsman's stoop.
Yet proved the most rewarding.

Perfect for its purpose,
holding an ample portion
measured most exactly,
pouring precise and full.

A fit vessel also
for vital decoration.
These marks of waves and footsteps
somewhere by the sea

—in fact a web of order,
each mark accommodating
the shapes of all the others
with none at fault, or false;

a system of live images
making increased response
to each increased demand
in the eye of the beholder,

with a final full response
over the whole surface
—a total theme—presented
to a full intense regard:

Nine waves out, a ship
lying low in the water,
battered from a journey,
the waves lapping around it

marked with the faint detail
of all the perils past.
A few firm footprints
emerging from the ocean

and planted on the seashore;
the sand grains shifted,
marked with the faint detail
of perils still to come.

Nine steps inland
where the two worlds meet, or divide,
a well of pure water,
with the first prints fading.'

He poured her a long portion
of the best blood brandy,
and lifted the brimming beaker
to her motherly regard.

'Remembering the Father,
His insult when offended,
our proneness to offend,
we will drink to His absent shade.'

A smile, dry and lipless
disturbed her stern features.
Her lean arms opened,
acknowledging her son.

He limped off leftward
topping up their glasses
along the head table,

and danced off downward
out among the others,
everyone in turn.

From Stephen's Green I turned my feet
contented into Grafton Street.

The walls obscured the sinking sun.
Warmth and certainty were gone.

*

A final turn, the scribal trades
appearing through the dusk . . .

    . . . their shades
restless, and a muffled roar
guides us to the very door

Outside, the spirit of the place,
the bar light flickering on his face,
haunts the gutter, sways and stoops
in rapt abandon, dives and swoops
with bow and fiddle—living things—
and, double-stopping, sweeps the strings
with passionate inaccuracy.

Inside: an overcrowded sty,
maroon in tone. Disputing hordes
mingle on the naked boards.
A spotted mirror, vast in size
and framed in bottles, multiplies
their slow turmoil. A chilly glaze
coats the lofty walls. A haze
of smoky light obscures the bar
where some of the more particular
have turned their backs.

                Three poets sprawl,
silent, minor, by the wall.
Locked in his private agony,

showing the yellow of his eye,
a ruined Arnold turns his face
snarling into empty space,
flecks of black about his lips.
Next, a ruined Auden slips
lower on the leather seat,
his tonsure sunken in defeat
—roused to fits and starts of life
by the distant shrilling of his wife.
Last, downcast and liquid-lipped,
umbrella handle moistly gripped
and staring inward, doomed and mild,
a ruined, speechless Oscar Wilde.

Standing apart, a group of two:
an ageing author passing through,
a giant bringing into town
an atmosphere of vague renown,
a female student, open-eyed,
held to his patriarchal side.
Once more, with slow authority,
he tells her how it came that he
was passed all day from hand to hand
by friends and brilliant strangers and,
stupefied from endless bars
and ever-changing private cars,
established insecurely here
before two flattened pints of beer.
He halts a moment, losing track.
His palm slips lower down her back.

Six or seven, more or less
connected with the daily press,
are gathered in the centre light
debating the subject for the night
—Drink and the High Creative Arts—
with a novelist from Northern parts
collecting data in the South.
With every word that leaves his mouth,
tiny, admiring, by his knee
a lecturer in history
agrees excited.

                    Off his beat
and growing feeble on his feet,
a civil servant holds his case
close in a desolate embrace:
once more passed over.

                            Young and lean
a new arrival on the scene,
bluff, direct, with candid eye,
agreeable, and keeping dry,
is balanced back upon his heels.
In from the provinces, he feels
at home at once, cuts short his chat,
polite, with the tragic bureaucrat,
and aims a grin across his head
at one that (he has heard it said)
writes leaders on the local news
and manages the book reviews.

*

A chorus of disgust draws all
attention toward the farther wall.
Hemmed in the thickest of the press,
arrayed in spattered sporting dress
and seized by total indignation,
shocked at his shameful situation,
rages ruined Anonymous.
'Is nothing ever serious?'
Students struggle for a place
with betting men before his face.
He showers with a scornful snort
Truth and Beauty on his court:
'God deliver me from you
good-for-nothing mocking crew
that only know to jeer at Joy.
When I was a growing boy
and bent my back in ditch and dung
it wasn't mockery that flung

329

my holy body down one day
in ecstasy upon the clay,
but Truth that ne'er obeyed the call
of witty intellectual
—the tragic thing that shames the jiber
and monthly magazine subscriber!'

With happy cheers the bar resounds:
'Phonies! Culchies! Dirty hounds!
But why are you so hard on *us*?
Forgive! Forgive! Anonymous!'

'I'm not in the unforgiving or
forgiving business any more,'
Anon replies. 'Accursed pity
I ever came to Dublin city,
packed my bag and left behind
the very source I came to find.
I'd more between my thumb and finger
any Summer night I'd linger
up against a wooden gate
in simple pleasure. Now, too late,
here in Hell I count the cost:
simple conviction that I lost
in bothering with Dublin's loud
self-magnifying, empty crowd.
—Double foolishness to flatter,
by attack, what doesn't matter.
But Time heals all and will produce
the only answer: What's the use?'

*

An acolyte with aching bladder
exits down a weeping ladder.
A dwarf official with a tray
collects and jingles on his way,
jams a while inside a pen
of duffle-coated racing men,
drops his eyes and whispers low:
'Excuse me, ladies.'

Time to go.
The hands are reaching half-past ten.
Last drinks are swiftly measured, then
the barman halts and, howling 'Please!',
reaches back and rasps his keys
across an iron grating—'Gents!'
A moment's hush: the air grows tense.
We lift our faces from the trough.
The house lights flicker on and off.

A consciousness of distant parts,
with resignation, fills our hearts.
Rising and starting on our way
with cries of sadness and dismay,
we exit, crowding toward a pair
of sighing barmen at the rere.
Two clerks in liberated sex
collapse across each others' necks.
Friends we had not seen before
struggle, joking, through the door
and mingle in the dirty lane.
The door is slammed; they draw the chain.
We feel the cold among the slops
of fish and meat and poultry shops,
shrug our shoulders, turn our backs
and face a line of bursting sacks.

Then start upon our various ways.
Someone, sick or singing, stays
bent or leaning by the wall,
mindless of our mocking call.
The back door opens, throws a ray
of smoky light across the way.
A man, with brush, behind our backs
sweeps our waste across our tracks,
wipes his feet and bolts the door
against us, and is seen no more.

The dark is kind, where day will bring
some dew-drenched, green, revolting thing.

Dream

Picture a stony desert, baked and still.

A creature scuffles among the rocks
and stops, harrying its own vitals.
Another figure stands still on one foot,
pulling its head down between its shoulders,
torn by a great extinct beak. Other shapes
are lying here and there in the dust.

A group of human figures makes an appearance,
some seemingly at home in the pitiless waste.
One of their number is smiling all around him.
With another, bolder than the rest,
he approaches the first two creatures,
misjudging their apparent preoccupation.
He is caught by the first and swallowed in an instant.
His companion is seized by the second as a support.
The others squat on their heels, watching and waiting,
opening their throats and wailing
with low voices.
                    The scene darkens.

Then brightens again. Three years—ten years—have passed.
The desert is full of voices, and blossoming.
A breeze ruffles a carpet of wild flowers.
The man-eater, in a ring of bones,
bares his yellow teeth. It is a smile.
He holds a bunch of coarse herbs up to his snout;
cassia, the purging flax.
                        The monopod,
decked in bittersweet from head to foot,
hops about, garrulous.
                        Most of the early group
have vanished. A few are lying still.
A hand—a voice—flutters among them vaguely.
Another group is gathering, exercising
new expressions and attitudes as they come,
in range from faded sneer to witless discovery.

The last I remember is a ring of these ghosts
surrounding the scene. One of them, seven feet tall,
prods at random with a shadowy stick.
There is some excitement in one corner,
but most of the ghosts are merely shaking their heads.

I left the road where a stile entered the wood,
the dry trees standing quiet in their own grain,
bare branches with sharp fingers out everywhere.

Faced suddenly with a mouse body
upside down, staring, on a patch of bark.
The shape small, the wings flat.

Meant only to be half seen
quick in the half light: little leather angel
falling everywhere, snapping at the invisible.

We sat face to face at the kitchen table
silent in the morning cold,
our bodies and body hair clean.

Outside, a faint coarse call
came from a throat high in the light
and higher up in the valley
a coarse quiet throat-answer

—our raven couple talking together,
flying up toward their place
on the high rock shoulder.

I have known the hissing assemblies.
The preference for the ease of the spurious
—the measured poses and stupidities.

On a fragrant slope descending into the fog
over our foul ascending city
I turned away in refusal,
and held a handful of high grass
sweet and grey to my face.

335

Note on Peppercanister Poems

Peppercanister was established in 1972 as a small publishing enterprise, with the purpose of issuing occasional special items from our home in Dublin, across the Grand Canal from St Stephen's Church, known locally as 'The Peppercanister'.

Butcher's Dozen was published in April 1972, a week after the report of the Widgery Tribunal of Inquiry into the shooting of thirteen civil rights demonstrators by the British Army in Derry on 30 January.

A Selected Life, published in July 1972, is a funeral poem written in memory of Seán O Riada, composer and musician, who died in October 1971. *Vertical Man* was published in August 1973 as a sequel to *A Selected Life*; it is set in Philadelphia on the first anniversary of O Riada's death.

The Good Fight was published in November 1973 for the tenth anniversary of the death of John F. Kennedy.

These four occasional poems were collected, with a commentary, in the book *Fifteen Dead* published by the Dolmen Press in 1979, in association with Oxford University Press. *Butcher's Dozen* was reissued at Easter 1992 for the twentieth anniversary of the Widgery Report.

A second series of Peppercanister publications consisted of two sequences, *One* and *A Technical Supplement*, published in 1976, and a group of poems published in 1978 as *Song of the Night and other poems*. These were collected in the book *One and Other Poems*, and published by the Dolmen Press with Oxford University Press.

Peppercanister publications have continued as a form of draft publication, distributed by the Dedalus Press, Dublin, and collected in the books *Blood and Family* (1988) and *From Centre City* (1994) by Oxford University Press.

OXFORD POETS

Fleur Adcock
Moniza Alvi
Joseph Brodsky
Basil Bunting
Tessa Rose Chester
Daniela Crăsnaru
Michael Donaghy
Keith Douglas
D. J. Enright
Roy Fisher
Ida Affleck Graves
Ivor Gurney
David Harsent
Gwen Harwood
Anthony Hecht
Zbigniew Herbert
Tobias Hill
Thomas Kinsella
Brad Leithauser
Derek Mahon
Jamie McKendrick

Sean O'Brien
Alice Oswald
Peter Porter
Craig Raine
Zsuzsa Rakovszky
Henry Reed
Christopher Reid
Stephen Romer
Carole Satyamurti
Peter Scupham
Jo Shapcott
Penelope Shuttle
Anne Stevenson
George Szirtes
Grete Tartler
Edward Thomas
Charles Tomlinson
Marina Tsvetaeva
Chris Wallace-Crabbe
Hugo Williams